MASTERPIECE

18 ENCOUNTERS WITH JESUS
THAT PROVE IT'S ALL ABOUT YOU!

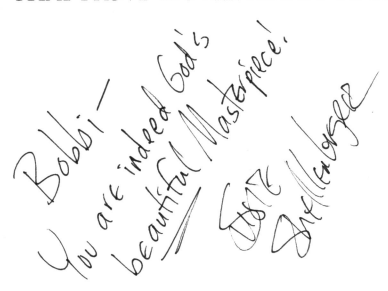

Bobbi —
You are indeed God's
beautiful Masterpiece!

Susie Shellenberger

SUSIE SHELLENBERGER | BILLY HUDDLESTON

Susie Shellenberger/Billy Huddleston

FaithHappenings Publishers
7061 S. University Blvd., Suite 307
Centennial, CO 80122

Cover design: Sherwin Soy

Book Layout: Sherwin Soy

Masterpiece © Susie Shellenberger/Billy Huddleston—1st edition

ISBN: Softcover 978-1-941555-02-6

This book was printed in the United States of America.
To order additional copies of this book, contact:
INFO@FAITHHAPPENINGS.COM

FaithHappenings Publishers,
a division of FaithHappenings.com

TABLE OF CONTENTS

CHAPTER 1: 12

Beginnings
(Mark 1:1)
Without a great foundation, the middle and end are shaky at best.

CHAPTER 2: 26

The Descender
(Mark 1:9-15)
What's in a name? Everything...if you're willing to live up to it.

CHAPTER 3: 40

Attached
(Matthew 4:18-22)
An invitation that can shatter the mundane. How will you respond?

CHAPTER 4: 54

True Authority
(Mark 1:21-28)
Jesus never cowers from confrontation. Whether it's good vs. evil;
beautiful vs. repugnant; authenticity vs. hypocrisy, He never cowers.

CHAPTER 5: 73

At Once
(Luke 4:38-41; Mark 1:29-31)
The Master Artist is at work. When He paints, He paints with urgency
and beauty.

CHAPTER 6: 91

Extreme Makeover
(Matthew 8:1-3; Mark 1:35-42)
Where do you go when you're broken, unwanted and ostracized? You
go to the One with open arms of healing, love and restoration.

CHAPTER 7: 104

Disobedience Costs
(Mark 1:43-45)
How often does disobedience matter? Always.

CHAPTER 8: 118
Get to Jesus
(Luke 5:17-39; Mark 2:1-4)
Jesus will do anything to reach you. What will you do to reach Him?

CHAPTER 9: 134
The First Word
(Mark 2:5)
To one who is devastated, inadequate, and lost...the first word is all that matters.

CHAPTER 10: 148
Forgiven
(Mark 2:1-5)
It's the most cherished word in the world.

CHAPTER 11: 158
From Their Hearts
(Mark 2-3:6)
How can one who hasn't been to art school create a canvas extraordinaire? It all depends on who holds the brush.

CHAPTER 12: 172
On the Move
(Matthew 9:9; Mark 2:8-14)
How far would you go to get a friend to Jesus?

CHAPTER 13: 186
No Plan B
(Matthew 9:9; Mark 2:13-14)
When the Master Artist invites you inside the canvas, it's for eternity.

CHAPTER 14: 199
Storms
(Mark 4:35-41; 6:45-53)
Gale-force winds, lightning strong enough to split a boat...we tend to focus on the storm. But the Master Artist is still focused on you.

CHAPTER 15: 215
Twelve Years
(Matthew 9:18-23)
Time. It's taken for granted—until it's you around whom the hands of
the clock revolve.

CHAPTER 16: 231
Get Outta the Graveyard
(Luke 8:26-39)
Sometimes we get so comfortable wearing shackles, we begin to
accessorize them.

CHAPTER 17: 245
Devastated but not Destroyed
(Luke 22:54-62)
When you're at the end of your rope, trust the One who's holding it.

CHAPTER 18: 264
Strange
(Mark 1:2-8)
Sometimes the least likely to win the race, get the lead in the play, and
are remembered forever.

INTRODUCTION

The paint is still wet on the canvas.
The colors glisten in the sun.
Texture and technique equal vibrancy extraordinaire.
The Artist has created brilliance.

But instead of putting down His brush, He waves it over His creation
and breathes directly into the painting. The colors receive His breath
and begin to move. Rhythm gives birth to shape. Silhouettes become
personalities. Life explodes through the canvas.

It's a masterpiece. What the Artist has captured is beyond your
imagination. You don't want to blink for fear of missing something.
As your focus intensifies...you're able to see beyond the kaleidoscope
of vivacity...and you're stunned.
You're looking at you.

The Artist has included *you* in His painting.
It's hard to swallow.
Your heart is racing.
How is this possible?
It may be hard to believe...
but breathe a sigh of relief, because it's true.

YOU are inside the greatest painting in the world.
In fact, even before the Artist picked up His brush,
you were on His mind.

He knew the color of your hair before He painted it.

He saw your laugh lines before sketching them.

He places so much value in who you are, that He never thought twice about placing you in His creation. In fact, if you look a little closer, you'll see a resemblance between you and the Artist.

He fashioned everything in this masterpiece after His own image.

YOU are in the painting.

YOU are part of the masterpiece.

YOU have reason to rejoice.

As you study the work before you, it begins to move...

You realize this is not a still painting.

It's a *moving* piece of art.

Let's not simply look at the painting or admire it from a distance.

Transformation never comes from simply viewing.

The Artist has extended His hand.

He has issued the invitation.

Will you join Him?

He invites you *inside* the masterpiece.

Go ahead.

Step inside.

Look around. Characters are moving swiftly now.

The Artist Himself is quickening. He's engaged. And He's moving more rapidly than anything else on the canvas.

What is He doing?

Look around.

MASTERPIECE

Notice every detail.
This is all about you.

Soak it in.
The Artist is shifting everything in the painting to get to you.
From His vantage point, it's *you* on center stage.
The painting revolves around you.
He's literally moving heaven and earth to get to *you*.
He's chasing you.
He wants you.
He's calling you by name.

Allow yourself to be captured.
Captivated by Him.

It's all about you.
If you were the only one in all the world to paint...
He'd still use the richest, most vibrant, all-expensive colors.
It's all about you.
You're the one for whom He died.
You're the one for whom He refused to stay in the tomb.
You're the one for whom He has purchased the new canvas.

You'll meet some fascinating personalities affected by the Artist.
You'll become part of the story inside the stories the Artist has breathed
onto the canvas.

Go ahead.
Accept His invitation inside the painting.
Discover your story by learning His.

Along the way, you'll engage in 18 encounters that prove
it really is
all about
you.

CHAPTER
ONE

We yearn for a good starting point, don't we?

An exciting entrance with a colorful invitation and a golden ticket ensures fascination.

Chances are, if the beginning is good, we'll stick with the story all the way to the end.

But without a great foundation, the middle and end are shaky at best.

THE BEGINNING
(Mark 1:1)

"It was the best of times; it was the worst of times."

"Once upon a time."

"He was an old man who fished alone."

"In the beginning, God..."

There's nothing more important than an opening line. It's a fact that every writer, composer and salesperson knows well.

What follows will succeed or fail depending on how good it begins. The story lives or dies. The song crescendos or deflates. The sale is confirmed or denied.

The greatest story...

the best composition...

the most exhilarating presentation...

is found in the opening line of the Bible. "In the beginning God created the heavens and the earth."

"In the beginning God." Let's stop here for a moment.

Do you catch the power in this lead sentence?

This is *the* opening line. The opening line to the most important story of all time; the story of the ages!

What captures your attention when reading these words?

First, we see that God Himself is the Author of this story: "In the beginning God." All focus is on Him. As Creator, Inventor and Flesh-Maker, He's center stage. As Father, Friend and Forgiver, He's on the front lines.

He's our starting point. The originator of *His*tory. It all begins with Him. His design. His plan. His creation. God is the Author of all. Your story is being written by Him. To learn more about *your* story, however, we first need to learn *His*tory. Throughout the story, the

Author reveals who He is.

He's an artist.

He's the Master Artist.

He takes a clump of dirt and paints life with it.

He winks and life is spread across the Creator's canvas.

He's intensely focused. He draws closer to the canvas and smiles.

YOU are His focus. Yes, it's you. You're on the canvas.

You're in the Master Artist's masterpiece.

He's Not Silent

In Genesis we discover a God who speaks. The Author has a voice! This is evidenced when we read the phrase, "And God said..." six times in the creation account.

His voice is powerful. When God speaks, things happen! For every "and God said," we have an "and it was so." He spoke—and it was.

He's still speaking. The issue: Are you listening? His voice is unmistakable. Look around you.

He speaks order out of chaos.

Substance out of emptiness.

Light out of darkness.

Something out of nothing.

Beauty out of ugliness.

Hope from despair.

Life out of lifelessness.

The Proof

We see the evidence of the power of His voice in Genesis 1:26-31 when He speaks man into existence. From a handful of dirt, God forms man. And He doesn't form man like He formed plant life or the animals. He creates man in His own likeness—in His own image!

Watch what God does next. He leans over and breathes His very breath into man's nostrils, and man becomes a living soul! He was shaped by goodness and declared good by God Himself. All that God created was good, but He declared man to be the masterpiece of His creation. Think of it: *You* are a masterpiece! You were created in beauty—in the image of the Master Artist Himself. You're on the canvas.

Created free, whole, complete…the masterpiece would enjoy life in all its fullness with his Maker. What a beginning!

The Action Continues

The story gets better. God actually speaks to His creation, and we hear the conversation:

"Of every tree you may freely eat,
but of the tree of the knowledge of good and evil you shall not eat, for in
the day that you eat of it you shall surely die"
(Genesis 2:16-17 NKJV).

"You are free," THAT'S what God says to man.

We're not really talking about dietary choices. We're talking about all the junk we deal with today—worry, sickness, fear, dread, aches, pains, desires, sorrow—you name it, man was completely free from all that.

Man and woman would enjoy a beautiful love relationship with their Creator in which every single one of their needs would be met. Adam and Eve would lack for nothing. They were free. They were complete. All they had to do was stay away from that one tree.

Important fact: Man was created to be God-centered. We were formed in His very image. Filled with His Spirit. We were created for relationship with Him and with each other.

But relationship goes two ways, right? In other words, forced relationship isn't really relationship at all. Our Creator longs for authentic love with His creation.

What would be the mark of true love? Obedience. "Eat from any tree...except one." Love God enough to live in response to His voice. Obey Him. This would result in a God-centered existence.

And Then...

Sadly, something goes terribly wrong with this perfect beginning. One day we see Eve standing next to the forbidden tree. Why is she there? Is she bored with all she *can* do and wants to compare it with what she's been told *not* to do? Doesn't she know she's on dangerous ground?

> *What would be the mark of true love? Obedience.*

Before we come down too hard on her, let's remember that there's a little Eve in all of us. How often do we simply want to see how close we can get to what's off limits?

I won't partake. I'll just take a look.

I won't stay. I'll just make an appearance.

We are not as strong as we think we are! We still suffer the effects of a fire without getting burned. That's the problem with getting too close.

Eve is too close. So it's no surprise that slithering around the forbidden tree is the enemy of the Creator.

The Deceiver.

The Father of Lies.

Satan himself.

He sings a delicious song. Temptation is veiled inside a pulsating melody beckoning Eve to join the dance. We stand near and watch closely. Every fiber of who we are desires to intervene, to warn, "No, Eve! It's a trick. Listen closer to the cadence. Something's wrong. The rhythm is off. It's not your melody. Eve, *your* song is lofty. Worthy of a symphony. The song you were created to sing is orchestrated with eternal love."

Satan's sour notes are masked by a heavy beat. The rhythmic vibration is tantalizing. Convincing. He sings a ballad of doubt—a chorus of confusion. Eve allows the aria to swell within. She now breathes the cadence becoming one with the rhythm. At this point, Eve can no longer discern between her Creator's song and the song of the Deceiver.

Crunch.

She bites.

And with the juice of the fruit dripping from her lips she turns to Adam and he eats.

The rhythm has stopped. The melody is gone. There *is* no song. Only thunder. And shame. And anger. And…what's happening? The trees are different. Flowers once blooming in vibrancy are now filled with thorns. All of creation mourns deeply.

Things have changed. Forever.

Adam and Eve have shifted from being God-centered, to self-centered. They'll have it their way. They'll rule themselves. By their actions, they have made the declaration: "We love ourselves more than we love our Creator."

Downward Spiral

This is the fall of creation. The paint on the Artist's canvas blurs. Now, for the first time, Adam and Eve experience what's behind the Deceiver's song: fear, guilt, shame, and bitterness. We're still hearing the same song today. It's a chorus of pornography, gambling, drunkenness. The verses boast eating disorders, an affair, low self-esteem and abuse. We're getting too close. Discernment is fading.

Adam and Eve hear God strolling through the Garden, and instead of running to their Creator as they always have, they hide instead.

First, they hide from each other.

Then they hide from God.

God, who formed them in His sacred image.

God, who filled them with His very Spirit.

God, who created them for love and relationship.

God, who made them to live in freedom.

God, who called them His masterpiece.

Love in Action

We're still standing by Eve, watching this nightmare. Look carefully now, because we're about to see one of the most beautiful pictures we have in scripture. Genesis 3:9 tells us that as God strolls through the garden, He calls to His creation: "Adam, where are you?"

We're getting too close. Discernment is fading.

This isn't a call of ignorance, nor is it a grandiose game of hide-and-seek. It's impossible to hide from God. Just listen to the words of the psalmist:

"Where can I go from Your Spirit? Or, where can I flee from Your Presence?"
(Psalm 119:7 NKJV)

Be sure this was not a call from God to find His creation. No, it's the exact opposite. He knew. That's why He called.

From Billy:

I've known Lynelle most of my life. Our moms have been friends even longer than we have. Lynelle and I went to the same high school, marched in the band together and rode to school together in Bobby Hinson's bright yellow Volkswagen van. We have some great memories!

Surprise!

In the late 90s, Lynelle met Jeremy at church. They hit it off quickly and were married on May 15,1999. The newlyweds moved into a house on Quatman Ave. What's really neat is that's the street where I live. Actually, we're neighbors. You can't ask for anything better than this—neighbors and friends.

Throughout the years the three of us have had many great times—and we're still making memories. I love having such close friends to travel with, laugh with and talk about God together. The three of us share so much in common.

A New Decision

Toward the end of 2000, Jeremy and Lynelle decided that it was time to start a family. It's something they longed for, really. Then, it happened. News came that Lynelle was expecting. It seemed like everything was falling into place. You could sense the excitement, the anticipation. All was right in their world. Until the word came. Shortly into their pregnancy, they received news that something wasn't right. Things weren't progressing and there were some issues. The ultimate nightmare for any expectant couple.

In February 2002, because of a genetic disease/issue they lost their child. Along with that loss it seemed as though hope vanished as well. Because of the genetic issue, the possibility of having a child of their own was gone.

Devastated, they went on. A funeral. A memorial garden in the backyard. All the hurts and questions. It seemed their dreams lay shattered at their feet. The excitement was gone. Now, they'd live under the cloud of this horrible reality.

Moving On

One night in 2004, Lynelle was awakened from a dream. A dream about China. A dream about a little girl. Through she felt as though God was placing upon her heart the longing to adopt, it was a delicate issue. The pain of their loss was still raw, so she waited for the perfect opportunity to approach the subject with Jeremy.

But while she was waiting, God was already working. Jeremy began to have the same dream, the same longing. They didn't hesitate. They started the process. They'd have a family of their own!

Maybe you've gone through this process. Or, perhaps you know someone who has. If not, let me tell you…it's not an easy thing. Paperwork. Mountains of forms to be filled, signed, submitted. Fees. It's a costly thing to take this step. Yard sale after yard sale, fundraiser after fundraiser…yet there was no cost too great. They paid the fees.

Home studies. Would they qualify? Were they fit parents? What would the home life be like? What do the neighbors (wink,

wink) have to say? The ball was rolling.

That was in 2004.

2005 came and went. 2006 no news. 2007…2008…2009, still no news. How could this process be taking so long? Wasn't it God that spoke this desire into their hearts? Had they heard wrong? Misunderstood?

Time Marches On

So much time passed, they had to refile paperwork. Along with the paperwork, fees—which meant more yard sales and fundraisers. Now, new home studies had to be done. A lot can change in nearly five years.

How would you have felt? Do you think you might have questioned yourself? Or God? Would you have lost hope? I hate to admit it, but I did. I thought maybe this was something that wasn't meant to be. But you can be sure, during times such as these, God is at work.

What we didn't realize was that on April 18, 2010 in Ningxia, China, she was born. A little baby girl in dreadful conditions: an unfit mother, an absentee father and an unloving home in a culture that didn't value little girls. So, being unwanted, this newborn baby was placed by her so-called mother in a ditch by the river to die.

Can it Get Any Worse?

I have to confess, that's hard to think about. It's difficult just to type. It's unimaginable. How could anyone do such a thing?

I'm not sure how long this child lay in the ditch. But as time passed, so did a stranger. Walking by the river one evening he heard a faint whimper, a tiny cry, a struggle for life coming from the weeds. Walking toward the sound, he found her: an unwanted, thrown away, barely living little girl. He refused to leave her in a ditch by the river.

He carried her to an orphanage where she would be cared for. An orphanage overrun by unwanted little girls, left in ditches and shoeboxes or trashcans. She wouldn't have her own bed. She'd be fed the minimum. She'd likely rarely be held. But, it was better than a ditch by the river.

Beauty From Ashes

Then it happened. In February 2011, the call came. There was a baby girl in Ningxia, China for Jeremy and Lynelle! Hope was renewed. Preparations were made. Then, on April 25th they claimed her as their own. And today Alyssa is my neighbor, too. In fact, we just celebrated her third birthday this past April 18th. By the way, did I mention that Jeremy's birthday is April 18th?

I'm usually home on Thursdays, and when I am, Jeremy and Lynelle set a place for me at their table. Little Alyssa has me wrapped around her finger. When I sit next to her, she looks up at me and says, "That's my Billy!" I don't have to tell you that my heart melts every time I hear that, do I?

I share this story to make this truth crystal clear: Adoption always starts in the heart of the parent. It wasn't Alyssa lying in a ditch by the river dreaming of Jeremy and Lynelle. It was the other way around. Now, she resides in their home on Quatman Avenue next door to me.

Alyssa is a *masterpiece.*

When mankind would never, could never, come to God, God would do the greatest thing imaginable. He would come to him. **He refused to leave them in their ditch!** The Creator pursues His creation. He goes to Adam and Eve so their relationship can be restored. It all began in the Father's heart. It was His desire.

He takes the initiative! He longs for that intended love relationship to be restored. He yearns for His children to be in His God-centered existence. He grabs fresh paint. The Artist is at work bringing restoration to His creation.

Do you realize that's the story of the Old Testament? It's the pursuit of a Holy God to an unholy people. It's the picture of a Creator who longs to be in relationship with His creation. This longing is so fierce that we see God—all through the pages of history—going to great lengths to bring people to Him.

Doesn't it seem outrageous?

A Creator God in contract with a created, fallen people?

Every single time, God keeps His end of the bargain.

Every single time, man breaks his word.

Restoration? Impossible.

At one with our Creator? Never going to happen.

It's hopeless. At least it seems that way.

When there seems to be no way, God does the greatest thing imaginable. He robes His Son in human flesh and sends Him from the ivory halls of heaven to be born on earth. Why?

To be one with His broken creation.

Relationship.

Love. It's what we were made for.

He grabs fresh paint. The Artist is at work bringing restoration to His creation.

From Heaven to Earth

Now in Jesus, we see that God

has invaded humankind. He has come to do for us what we could not, would not do for ourselves. This is His story. So, Mark makes the announcement:

> *"The beginning of the Gospel of Jesus Christ, the Son of God"*
> *(Mark 1:1 NKJV).*

This story is *of* Him. It originates with Him. It is derived of Him. It's composed of Him. He's the melody and the lyric. He's the good news.

But it *becomes* all about you. We'll see the Master Artist re-arrange everything on His canvas just to get you in the center.

It's a story that started long ago. This was the plan from before time began. It's a plan from the heart of the

He still brings order out of chaos.

Creator who longs to be in relationship with His creation so much so, that He'll provide the way!

The Gospel is Alive

It's an exciting story!

In Jesus, we see a God who still speaks: We hear His voice as He speaks to us.

In Jesus, we see a God who is still active: He still brings order out of chaos, light out of darkness, something from nothing, beauty out of ugliness, hope from hopelessness, life from lifelessness.

Jesus came so there might be a Gospel!

What a story.

What a lead sentence.

What an opening line. And think, it's just beginning.

Going Deeper

(To be answered individually or with a small group.)

- What are some great opening lines—or lead sentences—you'll never forget?
- How does it make you feel to know that God sees YOU as His masterpiece? What are some ways your lifestyle reflects being made in His image?
- What are some of the most common temptations you face?
- Read 1 Corinthians 10:13. Write this Scripture on a card and strive to memorize it. How can the truth from this Scripture help you fight the Enemy when he tries to deceive you?
- Can you identify with Jeremy and Lynelle? Have you longed for something, had your hopes dashed, longed again, and finally the dream came true? Or perhaps the dream died. Describe the emotional roller coaster. What did you do during this time to keep your faith strong?
- God's greatest desire is that you live in wholeness—in completion—with Him. What would this look like in your life?

Prayer time: Dear Father, I yearn to be one with You. Help me to take advantage of Your way out the next time I'm tempted. Thank You for the exciting beginning You have in store for me!

CHAPTER
TWO

Sometimes, though we're on top of the world,
we find the earth beneath us falling apart.
When we fall, we often fall long and hard.
But there's hope!
You don't have to stay down.
Your best days haven't been seen yet.

What's in a name?
Everything…if you're willing to live up to it.

THE DESCENDER
(Mark 1:9-15)

We're fascinated with names, aren't we? Walk into any gift store, and you'll find plaques with names and their meanings on them. When parents find out they're having a baby, one of the first things they do is start tossing around names. Baby name books are big sellers. It seems important we find the right name and the right meaning.

By the way, Billy means *determined protector*. Susie means *lily*. Nothing fancy, but at least they're not weird. Check this name out:

Brfxxccxxmnpccccllllmmnprxvclmnckssqlbb11116

A Swedish couple gave it to their newborn baby boy. They pronounced it: Albin. The court rejected the name and made the couple pay a fine for wasting legal time. The couple then changed the name to A. This was also pronounced Albin. It was *also* rejected by the court.

On his first passport, the boy's name was printed: "Ickenamngivetgossebarn," which means "unnamed little boy."

We find some interesting names throughout the Bible. Jacob means "Heelgrabber." He was Esau's twin and was born with his hand on his brother's heel. Esau was born with thick hair, and you guessed it, Esau means "hairy."

Any guesses to what the Jordan River's name means in Hebrew? The Descender.

Seriously. That's the Hebrew meaning of the Jordan River. It was named this because that's what it does—it descends. Rapidly.

Three streams spring out of the snows that rest upon the sky-high tops of mountains, and merge some 250 feet above sea level at the base of Mount Hermon, to form this river that's different from any other river in the world. At its origin the waters are said to be crystal clear. It starts its journey madly rushing through the narrow and ever-descending valley.

The Jordan River is filled with life.

Its beginnings are lofty.

Its end is low.

Very low.

It descends to nearly 1,300 feet below sea level and loses itself in the lap of death: The Dead Sea.

It starts high and is pristine.

It ends low, filled with the filth of the earth.

By the time The Descender reaches the Dead Sea it's a vile, filthy mess. It runs through a deep valley where it becomes nothing more than a muddy stream between two banks of mud to an extremely hot, dry, dead place.

A journey from beautiful mountain heights to a desolate wasteland.

It's The Descender.

From Billy:

In 2005, I was on top of the world. Everything seemed to be going my way. At 33, I'd been married for seven-and-a-half-years, had a beautiful townhouse on a golf course, a lovely wife, two dogs, and a bright future. Everything seemed to be falling in place.

Professionally, I couldn't have imagined things would be going as well as they were. I had entered the field of fulltime evangelism a number of years before, and God was blessing. My schedule was always full, and I was getting invited to do things I never would have dreamed possible.

I could see God's hand all over my life. I was in His plan

doing what He had called me to do. How could things be any better? I was on the mountaintop looking forward, but the rug of my world would soon be yanked from under my feet.

The year was coming to an end, and so was my revival schedule. It was the second week of December and I was in Richfield, Pa., preaching the last revival before Christmas break. I was looking forward to my time at home. It had been a good year, but even good years can be tiring!

When my wife and I married, we traveled together for the first three years. Life on the road can be tough. Living out of a suitcase is hard. She was interested in beginning a career, so we made some changes and decided she'd stay home. She was talented, intelligent, proficient, and ultimately successful. Again, everything seemed to be going our way.

Shocking News

Most of our lives were spent apart. When you live apart, you have to find and make ways to carry on a relationship. We'd talk on the phone everyday. Sometimes many times throughout the day.

It was Saturday. One more day and I would be heading home for two weeks. I remember talking to her that afternoon before the evening service. We were both anticipating I'd be home soon. Everything seemed fine. I headed out to service and had a great evening. Again, God was blessing.

When I returned to my room that night, I tried to call home. My wife was going to a Christmas party at her work, and I wanted to ensure she'd gotten back safely.

No answer. *That's OK. Nothing serious, I'm sure. She just hasn't made it home yet.* A little time passed and I called again.

Still no answer. Now I'm starting to get that sick feeling in my stomach. Something wasn't right. *I hope she's not in a ditch somewhere.* I prayed nothing horrible had happened. *I'll try again in a bit. I'm over-reacting.*

Again, no answer.

Time passed and my mind rolled. It was now around 4 a.m. Something was wrong. I dialed her sister; maybe she knew.

Then, I heard my wife's abrupt voice on the other end of her sister's phone, "I don't want you to come home."

The Descent

Everything came crashing down around me. How could this be? I'm on top of the world. This doesn't happen to me.

I was caught completely off guard. Don't get me wrong; it wasn't as though we didn't have any disagreements or discussions and even arguments. All married couples do. But it just wasn't supposed to happen like this.

Everything was moving in a foggy slow motion. I called the pastor of the church where I was speaking. He unlocked the door so I could load my sound system and product table. I needed to get home. Everything had changed.

My world lay shattered at my feet. I'd lost it all. My wife. My home. My ministry.

I now understood what it meant to be at the highest point and fall to the lowest.

I'm thankful Jesus refused to leave me there, and when I didn't have the strength to reach up, He came and lifted me.

My story doesn't end here; I'll share more, later.

And...Action!

The Jordan is also the sacred river of Scripture. It's right here—at this very river—that we read of the miracles of Elijah and Elisha, mighty prophets of old. The Jordan River provides believers with many benefits.

It's in the Jordan that Naaman—commander of the Syrian armies—dips seven times to be cured of the terrible disease of leprosy.

It's at the Jordan, the children of Israel, led by Joshua, cross to enter into the Promised Land.

It's where we meet John the Baptist.

It was on the banks of the Jordan he spoke the words:

"There comes One after me who is mightier than I..."
(Mark 1:7 NKJV).

It's this place where he was calling the people to come.

To repent.

To be baptized.

To prepare.

It's at this place where we meet Him.

God is at work. There's no question about this. It's reality. In chapter 18, we'll hear the words of the prophets (Malachi and Isaiah)—we'll be on the front row of earth's theatre.

These two Old Testament prophets will stand on stage left and stage right of history and announce John the Baptist.

We'll watch as he will momentarily take center stage in the wilderness and play his role with expertise.

We hear him as the voice of the forerunner.

We see him as the scout.

We know he's the footman.

We applaud him as he prepares the way.

Suddenly we read in Mark 1:9:

"Jesus came..."

Finally! This is what we've been waiting for. The main Actor steps into the drama of Mark's story. The spotlight is brighter than we've ever seen it shine. He comes!

But why here? Of all the places for Him to appear... a dry, hot, dead place? Incredible.

This is certainly not the grand entrance we expected. The anticipation is building for the main Actor to take the stage. We've been wondering who would fill the role.

What would He look like?

What would He sound like?

What's His name?

It's been building since the beginning.

Then, we meet Jesus.

A Man with a common name. You might expect something more; perhaps a little creativity. This Man comes from a common place: a town called Nazareth.

John baptizes Him. It doesn't go as smoothly as expected. John argues with Him about the whole thing.

Nazareth? Definitely not chic. Certainly not cosmopolitan. In fact, it would be asked, "Can anything good come from Nazareth?" That's really not a question. It's more of a statement dripping with sarcasm. It's an assertion, because Nazareth is just a common town.

To top it off, we see this common Man, from a common town, participating in a common experience. It's what everyone else was doing. They were making preparations for Him. John baptizes Him. It doesn't go as smoothly as expected. John argues with Him about the whole thing. (Check out Matthew's account of the event in chapter three.) It's all pretty common. Yet, He's the Star.

Why would He appear like this?

Really, what's going on here?

Why would Jesus be baptized?

What's the statement that's being made?

Supreme Plan

It's all about identity. We all want to be identified with something. People go to great lengths to identify themselves with the home team. We buy certain name brands to make fashion statements. We buy CDs, DVDs, decals for our car, and on and on and on. We long for identification.

From Susie:

I love Coca-Cola. In fact, sometimes I've wondered if my name really means "Coca-Cola" instead of lily. I have a loft upstairs in my home that I've transformed into a Coca-Cola café complete with: Coke booths, chairs, round tables, tall pub tables, rotating Coke lights hanging from the ceiling, animated Coca-Cola signs, a 1950s Montgomery Wards' Coca-Cola cooler that holds my Coca-Cola dinnerware, a 1917 restored Coca-Cola cash register, 1970s Coca-Cola Vendo machine (you get little bottles of ice-cold Coke for a dime!), a Coca-Cola ceiling fan, a Coca-Cola counter—and holding up the counter is a three-rowed, lighted-mirror-backed wall of empty Coca-Cola bottles. On the other side of the Coke counter, you'll find the stovetops, grill, griddle, sink, and fridge.

Walk down the hall with me to my guest room and you'll see a small red-and-white Coca-Cola table with red-and-white striped chairs, the bed has Coca-Cola sheets, and the guest bathroom has Coca-Cola towels, waste can and washcloths. Going down the hall, you'll notice shelves of cans and bottles from around the world with Coca-Cola written in various languages.

Is there any question that I love Coca-Cola? I have gone to great lengths to identify myself with the brown, sugary liquid that has the ever-so-slight sting right in the middle of its way down my throat.

When Jesus submits Himself to baptism, He identifies Himself with John. He knew the plan. Jesus knew John was the forerunner. In this recognition he realized He and John were one in the unfolding plan of God. They both had a role to play in the Divine Drama:

John came.

Jesus came.

In other words, He was giving credibility not only to the plan, but to the authenticity of John's role. It was a sign that the 400-year silence between the Old and New Testaments had been broken by a genuine voice from God. The Old and New were being brought together. God's plan was being fulfilled.

Not only did Jesus identify Himself with John, but also in His baptism, we see that He identifies with God, the Father. God's people had been longing for an authentic voice—for the silence to be broken. They believed God would break the silence.

So, they prayed.

And, they prayed.

Then they prayed some more:

"Oh, that You would rend the heavens! That You would come down!
That the mountains might shake at Your presence—"
(Isaiah 64:1 NKJV).

They'd been taught through the prophets that a special anointing would be upon the Promised Messiah to empower Him for His ministry. At the baptism, it was fulfilled:

"And immediately, coming up from the water, He saw the heavens parting and
the Spirit descending upon Him like a dove. Then a voice came from heaven, 'You
are My beloved Son, in whom I am well pleased'"
(Mark 1:10-11 NKJV).

Jesus identifies Himself with God, the Father. God identifies with the Son in His words of approval: He's well pleased. He's endued with power from the Spirit. The main Actor is going to take center stage!

His identification doesn't stop there. He's identified with John, the plan and the Father. This is all exciting. But, there's more.

Why would a common man, with a common name come to a common place to participate in a common experience?

So that He could identify with us!

It All Fits Together

That's why The Jordan, The Descender, is significant. It has to be so much more than just geography. Remember man's intended place?

Why he was created? How he was created?

In God's image.

Filled with God's spirit.

For a beautiful, God-centered existence.

That's pretty lofty. You could say that's living at the top of the mountain. That's where it started. But when sin occurred—when man disobeyed—he fell.

Really far.

Very quickly.

He was the original descender.

From pristine heights to a pool of death.

No hope of life ever springing forth.

Until, He comes. Christ steps into the stream of humanity and reveals to us what life is all about. He identifies Himself with us. The Master steps into the stream. He's baptized. He's approved of and empowered for life and ministry.

We see that played out on the street in Mark 1:12-13. Right after Jesus enters the stream of humanity, the battle is on. Jesus is thrust by the Spirit into the desert. It's a hot, wild, miserable place. Mark tells us Jesus was with the wild beasts. A place of death, destruction, isolation except for wild beasts, but it gets worse:

> *The Master steps into the stream. He's baptized. He identifies Himself with us.*

"He was there in the wilderness forty days, tempted by Satan"
(Mark 1:13 NKJV).

The same enemy that slithered around a tree in the Garden of Eden now slithers into the desert to confront our Star. Jesus has chosen to identify Himself with man in every way. The battle begins. But, He

doesn't fall! He stands against the enemy of the ages! He is victorious!
Our Master has chosen to place Himself as a common man with a
common name from a common town inside our common world to be
with His masterpiece.

Amazing.

Changes

With the entrance of our Star, we also see an exit. John the
Baptist is put in prison. We'll catch glimpses of him in some of the other
gospel accounts, but now he bows out. He has fulfilled the role and has
done an amazing job. His role was to point to Him—the Star. John has
played his part well. He has pointed to a common Man with a common
name from a common town with an uncommon message:

*"The time is fulfilled, and the kingdom of God is at hand.
Repent, and believe in the gospel"
(Mark 1:15 NKJV).*

The reality is: Man was created for relationship with the Creator.
He fell when he disobeyed, sinned in the garden. It was a fast descent,
the original descender. When there was no farther to fall, Jesus came.
He came as a man—to do for man—what man couldn't do for himself.
When there was no way to ever ascend to the heights of our intended
state, He came and made a way.

He identified Himself with us. He has ushered in the kingdom
and invited us to be a part. He has shown us the possibilities of life with
the Father: a return to a God-centered life from the muck and mire of a
self-centered existence that only leads to death.

This is reality: Jesus came.

The Master came from the highest and willingly descended to the lowest, simply to save, identify and restore His masterpiece.

Going Deeper

(To be answered individually or with a small group.)

- Do you know the meaning of your name? What does it mean?
- Are there some teams or labels with which you've identified yourself? How do you show your identification? (Susie built a Coca-Cola café, others wear jerseys, etc.)
- Describe a time when someone helped you out of a desperate situation. How did you feel? How did you display your gratitude?
- How does it make you feel to know that Christ, our Master, chose to step inside the dirty stream on the Jordan River to join humanity?
- How does your lifestyle reflect the identity of Christ?

Prayer time: Thank Christ for His willingness to come. Tell Him you're grateful He left the perfection of the highest, and willingly descended to the lowest just to identify and save us.

CHAPTER
THREE

Ever feel as though you're trapped in a cycle?

The same ol' same ol'?

There's not much meaning in redundancy.

It's tough to find purpose in the ordinary.

God issues an invitation that can shatter the mundane.

How will you respond?

ATTACHED

(Matthew 4:18-22)

Ahhh, the benefits of water.

We drink it. Cook with it. Jet-ski on it. Bathe in it. Para-sail over it. Surf through it. Wash clothing in it. Spend money to cruise through it.

Great cultures throughout history claim it.

Most large cities have it.

People thrive with it.

Large bodies of water: lakes, rivers, the ocean, and of course, the sea. We need these expansions of water to live. In fact, it's so important to our survival that about 70 percent of the earth is covered with it.

Let's focus specifically on the sea. It's a place of commerce. The sea is a means of travel, and a method of exporting and importing. In Scripture, almost every major biblical event occurs near water. This is where we find people. This is where the action is. Most of Jesus' ministry occurred by the Sea of Galilee. To say it's merely important is a huge understatement.

The Sea of Galilee is the largest body of fresh water in this area. It's nearly twelve-and-a-half miles long by seven-and-a-half miles wide. If you were to take an aerial shot of this sea, it would appear to be a basin of water surrounded by mountains. This is the location of our scene today. And proof that from God's point of view it's all about you.

Could Have Been a Monday

It was just another ordinary day.

Cast the net. Draw the net.

Cast the net. Draw the net.

The rhythm was seared inside their bones.

It's what they did. It's how they made their living.

It was an honorable trade with honest labor. They'd make their way through life by the strength of their backs and the sweat of their brow. They were fishermen. This was their routine. And, today was just another day… at least that's how it began.

But what these men of the sea—Simon and Andrew—didn't know was that today would be anything but ordinary. For in the midst of their routine they would have an encounter that would change their lives forever.

Cast the net. Draw the net.

Cast the net. Draw the net.

Cast: It's what they were doing when Jesus saw them.

It's interesting that's how it starts.

He saw them.

The language is very specific:

"And Jesus, walking by the Sea of Galilee, saw two brothers, Simon called Peter, and Andrew his brother, casting a net into the sea; for they were fishermen"
(Matthew 4:18 NKJV).

In the average, ordinary, mundane routine of life, Jesus went to them. Don't let this discovery escape your attention. It's not Simon and Andrew seeking Jesus in that moment. Instead, it's the pursuit. It's the story that has been played out time and again.

The Savior comes to you.

We serve a God who pursues. He chases. He's willing to move heaven and earth to have you as His own.

This is what sets Him apart from all other gods. Buddhists, Hindus, Islamists—and those who walk in all other faiths—work extremely hard to reach up. To grasp their god. They go to incredible extremes to find him.

Jehovah God, the *I AM*, the God of Moses and Abraham, the God speaking, living and breathing through every page of the Bible, is the God who through His Son, Jesus Christ, reaches down to you. Look closely. He's running toward you. He pursues you!

Think About It

These fishermen are average, hardworking guys.

Men who smelled of sweat and fish.

Guys with calloused fingers—each callous declaring its own story dictated by the sea.

They had rope-burned hands.

Sun-baked skin.

These guys had not attended an Ivy League school, or for that matter, any institution of higher education. They probably never made a splash outside of fishing. You wouldn't remember them at a high school reunion. They wouldn't have stood out in any crowd. They were fishermen. Nothing more, nothing less.

They were fishermen. Nothing more, nothing less.

There's no shame in that.

But simply put: This was their identity.

Yet, these are the guys whom Jesus pursues.

Jesus saw Simon and Andrew by the sea, where commerce is going on, with travelers going to and fro. In the midst of all the activity of everyday life by the Sea of Galilee, *He saw them.* Could it be that's why He went there that day? *He sought them.* Out of all the other people, He saw Simon and Andrew. Casting the net, drawing the net, casting… He initiates the encounter.

Then, He stops before them and speaks:

"Follow Me"
(Matthew 1:19 NKJV).

Command and Response

It seems a little odd doesn't it? Really. To stop before two guys, working hard at their daily routine, is strange enough, but to call them away? This is who they were. This is how they made their living. This is where they found their importance, their identity. However, this is the invitation: Jesus says, "Follow."

That's heavy. Partly because it's a command. The nature of a command is this: It demands response.

Christ's invitational command will either be answered with obedience or disobedience.

They'll either follow, or they'll continue to fish.

It's heavy, because at its nature, it's a command.

And what adds to the weight is what this will mean for Simon and Andrew.

Understand: This is not a simple invitation. It's not delivered on glossy cardstock decorated with cool graphics and a dated R.S.V.P. Jesus isn't inviting the brothers for a java break or a shared meal. This isn't even a weekend retreat or a business seminar.

This was a call from their routine. It was to step away from the ordinary—from life as they knew it.

It was an invitation for a new identity.

It was an invitation for a new identity.

What was Jesus inviting them to? What would following Him mean? How would their lives change? What about their occupation?

And why is it important that we answer these questions? It's because He's extending the same invitation to us, and we too, need to consider the depth of what this entails.

From Susie:

For the past two decades, I've taken groups of students and adults on two-week international mission trips every summer. Most of the time I take around 300, but there have been a few years we've had 500, 700, and one year, a little more than 800. It's a true adventure!

Big World Ventures, in Tulsa, Okla., custom designs each trip for me and handles the logistics of air travel, lodging, planning our daily ministry schedule, recruiting international pastors and translators, chartering buses, etc., so I don't have to worry about the details and can concentrate on what I love most: ministry.

We call the trips "Never the Same," because you truly are *never the same* afterward. They're unlike any other missions' trip. They're truly a unique combination of elements that would remind you of camp, missions, adventure, and genuine revival. We do a rotation of ministry: We present the Gospel through a 22-minute drama pantomime. This way, no one has to learn a foreign language. It's all set to Spanish narration and music, and each team has their own portable battery-operated sound system. So we can be *anywhere* and present the message of salvation. We never have to worry about an electrical outlet.

We also work with orphans and do work projects—painting churches, hauling brick—whatever the local churches need us to do. At the end of the day, everyone returns to our hotel for a hot meal and our own evening service that I call FUAGNEM (Fired Up And Going Nuts Every Minute!).

During this time, students share what they experienced during the day, Christian artists lead us in praise and worship, and I speak. (If you're interested in participating, go to: www. neverthesamemissions.org for more information).

I share the above to set the stage for what I *really* want you to know. It was a hot day in Guatemala. We were probably an hour outside of Guatemala City. Team three had their ministry list and had already presented the gospel drama in two villages and rejoiced at seeing so many villagers accept Christ as their Savior.

Their next stop? An open-air market. They climbed off the bus in their drama costumes and immediately started drawing a crowd. In the midst of vendors and daily shoppers, they squared-off enough space to begin the drama.

We couldn't help but notice a Guatemalan man making a deal in the busy marketplace. He placed several bills in the hand of a pimp and quickly grabbed the arm of a prostitute. After making his way toward the center of the market, he was stopped by the music and action of the drama.

He held tightly to the arm of the woman he had purchased, but it was evident that he was absorbing the message of the drama. He watched intently as Toymaker—symbolizing God—sent His only Son to save the toys (His creation) from the destruction they had brought on themselves.

He saw Toymaker crucified, and he smiled from ear to ear when he saw death conquered when He rose again.

When the drama concluded, many of our students gave their testimonies through the interpreter. The Guatemalan man stayed and listened. When the invitation was given to the crowd for anyone who would like to have their sins forgiven, he came forward and said, "I want that. I'm a sinner and I want eternal life in Jesus."

The interpreter prayed with him, and he asked Christ into his life. He confessed his sins and accepted Christ's authority to save him.

He then turned to his "purchased prize" and said, "Now that I'm following Christ, I can no longer do the things I've done. Please forgive me for wanting to use you. I have a new life now." He placed several bills in her hand and said, "This should pay for your cab ride home and the rest of your day."

This Guatemalan man recognized the authority of His Master. He was now a masterpiece, and in excitement, he detached himself from his old way of life and attached himself to all he could become in Christ's power.

What does the invitation to follow Him mean? For Simon and Andrew it would mean that as Christ's masterpiece, they would walk with the Master. They would become like Him. And Jesus was inviting them to walk with Him, not for the afternoon, but for life.

It would begin with the next three years: They would walk with the Master who invited them. They would have the opportunity to hear His voice, learn His views, watch His ways.

They would see how Jesus responded politically and mirror His example in giving to the government what was owed.

They would watch Him pray directly to the Father God—and would be taught how to do the same.

They would discover His authority against Satan and hear

Christ speak directly to the minions of evil, casting them out of people desperate for normalcy. And they would rejoice in having that same authority.

They would hear His every sermon and ponder, discuss and apply.

They would observe His emotions—admiration for a widow giving all she had, the pure joy with children of all ages, anger at those who desecrate the Temple, grief at the death of a friend, compliance with His mother's request for wine at a wedding, His loyalty in saying He'd never forsake them.

He summons us to a changed life.

They would see bread multiply, death defeated, disease vanish, sins forgiven. And eventually they would even duplicate the miracles of their Master.

Again, it was an invitation to walk with Jesus. To know Him. To fall in love with Him. To become one with their Master.

The Invitation Above All Invitations

It's important we understand the depth of this invitation. Christ isn't offering a part-time proposition. He summons us to a changed life. Within this invitation is a call. Within the call is a command. Within the command is action: "Detach yourself from the average, the ordinary, the routine, the mundane, and attach yourself to Me. Walk with Me. Learn of Me. Get to know Me. Fall in love with Me."

The story gets even more incredible. How is that possible? After Jesus gives the command, the invitation, He qualifies the command with a promise. It's really a conditional statement.

If...

Then...

If you'll do this, then I'll do this. You're familiar with that type of language. Listen to what He says:

> "...and I will make you fishers of men"
> (Matthew 4:19 NKJV).

So, in other words, Jesus is saying, "If you'll do this, then I will do a work in you. Your job is simply to respond. Then, in your response, I'll enable you to become all I created you to be.

Do you see it?

Cast the net. Draw the net.

Cast the net. Draw the net.

"Follow Me, and I will shatter the routine. I will make, I will do, I will produce, I will accomplish, I will form, I will fashion, I will cause you to come into a new state of being, a whole new way of living, from one level to the next. I will move you from the routine mundane to complete transformation."

But remember His promise? He'll do the work. All they have to do is respond. Detach and attach.

Detach from the ordinary.

Attach to the extraordinary.

Celebrate!

This is an invitation void of pressure! You find no need to push to perform, no struggle to measure up. He'll do the work. He'll bring it to fruition. He'll shatter the routine, chase away the mundane. It's all in response to Him.

There's a difference in someone who stares at the score and pounds the notes on a keyboard, versus the composer whose music flows unceasingly from the heart. *That's* the kind of difference we're talking about. That's the quality of invitation Jesus is offering.

Transformation.

No longer ordinary; extraordinary.

No longer basing their identity in what they do, but in whom they're attached.

Again, Christ's desire is to shatter their routines. He yearns for them to live a life of responding. In that responding He will do the work.

What work? The transformation within.

You see, He has big dreams for them. But it's not just them! He wants the same for *you*. He yearns to guide you away from the temporary earthly things from which you identify and to distinguish you with all that's eternal.

Back to the Invitation

So, what's the response of these fishermen? How do Simon and Andrew answer? Remember, it's an invitation coated with a command.

> *"They immediately left their nets and followed Him"*
> *(Matthew 4:20 NKJV).*

What? Immediately? We get the sense that there wasn't any time or effort to make a list of pros and cons. Is it hard to believe there wasn't any talk about a salary package or benefits? There wasn't even the question of where they were going to walk!

Attached to Jesus.
What a way to live!

They just followed Him with the promise He would move them from one level to the next. They trusted He would shatter their routines and define their lives by His presence. They simply believed Him.

SUSIE SHELLENBERGER | BILLY HUDDLESTON

Attached to Jesus. What a way to live!

The story repeats itself with two more fishermen that day: James and John, two more brothers.

He sees them.

He calls them.

They follow.

They leave the old life to step into the new.

They move from routine to response.

Life would never be the same.

Cast the net. Draw the net.

New strength gained. Purpose in His name.

Your Response

The invitation isn't outdated. It's as fresh today as it was the day it was first delivered to those around the Sea of Galilee. Christ comes to *your* life—wanting to shatter *your* routines. Instead of finding your identity in your career, your spouse, your looks, your talent, your family, He wants you to be identified in Him.

What would happen if you genuinely attached your very self to Him? The masterpiece cementing itself to the Master. And instead of trying to become all He wants you to be, what if you simply surrendered all, and let Him do the transformation within you?

You would never be the same.

Going Deeper

(To be answered individually or with a small group.)

- What are some common things in which we tend to place our identity?
- What do the following Scriptures have to say about being identified in Christ? John 1:12, John 15:15, 1 Corinthians 6:17, 1 Corinthians 6:19-20.
- Why do we sometimes struggle with letting go of our routine to accept Christ's invitation to become transformed?
- What does a life look like that's truly defined by Christ?
- Is there anything in your life that's keeping you from being totally defined by Him? If so, are you willing to leave that behind in your pursuit of following Him?

Prayer time: "Father, I invite You to shatter my ordinary routine. I want to follow You in every area of my life. Help me to trust You to do the transforming work within that needs to happen for me to become all You dream for me."

CHAPTER
FOUR

Have you experienced the power of Christ?

It's astonishing, isn't it?

To see the same power that created the universe in action today truly takes our breath away.

He's still moving in power, and He wants to empower you to do the *same*.

Jesus never cowers from confrontation.

Whether it's good vs. evil; beautiful vs. repugnant; authenticity vs. hypocrisy, He never cowers.

TRUE AUTHORITY
(Mark 1:21-28)

The village is unmistakably quiet. The market—usually buzzing with vendors—is empty and still. There are no children chasing each other or playing games of Hide-and-Seek. The small herd of goats usually crossing the street about this time is absent from the public.

Even the sea refuses to speak.

No one is fishing. Boats have retired at bay.

The only action near the shore is the gentle sway of the water.

The tax collector's booth displays a "CLOSED" sign in faded paint and hanging slightly crooked.

Today is the Sabbath.

The day of rest has arrived, and it's welcomed. It's a day of worship.

It's a day to...

Cease.

Desist.

Remember.

A call to cease from labor,

desist from ordinary work,

a call to remember what God has done.

Remember creation, remember redemption.

The Sabbath is a day to renew hope.

It's a day of peace in the turmoil of life.

It's necessary.

It's needed.

How do we know? God Himself established this day.

"By the seventh day God had finished the work he had been doing; so on the seventh day he rested from all his work. Then God blessed the seventh day and made it holy, because on it he rested from all the work of creating that he had done"
(Genesis 2:2-3 NIV).

Cease. Desist. Rest. Worship. That was the plan from the beginning. God would rest from His labor on the seventh day, the last day of the week.

Man would worship God on his first day of existence. He would start his life by enjoying God's presence; resting in His presence.

Enjoying Him.

Worshipping Him.

True peace.

Sabbath.

Crucial

The Sabbath is a big deal. The Jewish people went to great lengths to maintain the Sabbath. They would need a place to gather, to enjoy their God's presence; to worship. So they established the synagogue.

That's what the synagogue was intended to be—a gathering place for the Jewish people. It's where they would come to confess their faith to the One True God. It was a place that would be filled with prayers, Scripture reading, worship and teaching. It was the central aspect to Jewish life.

God was worshipped.

God's law was read.

His ways were proclaimed.

That's why Jesus is there today.

*"Then they went into Capernaum, and immediately on the Sabbath
He entered the synagogue and taught"
(Mark 1:21 NKJV).*

Jesus, the Master Artist, is announcing the Kingdom!

He has new brushes and bright paint.

He announces it to the faithful in the synagogue.

It's why He came. And they were ready to hear.

Let's jump inside the scene itself. Let's get inside the canvas to see the response of the people who were there that day and heard Jesus.

Imagine being with those who would hear first-hand the Kingdom proclaimed!

We can look into their eyes, read their facial expressions, notice their body language. Can you sense the excitement? Do you see their jaws on the ground? It's almost as though we can read their lips and hear their voices as they say something like, "What in the world did we just hear? We've never heard anything like this before! This man actually sounds as though He knows what He's talking about! He has such authority."

From Susie:

I was speaking at a youth retreat. God was moving. Students were responding to the message by coming forward and giving Christ absolute authority in their lives. After the service ended, the room cleared for the next activity. Some of the youth leaders were still there, and I noticed a high school girl sitting alone. She wanted to talk.

I sat next to her, and a few of the youth leaders joined me. "My name is Crystal," she said. "I want that. I need to pray."

"Hi, Crystal," I responded. "I'm glad you want to ask Jesus to forgive your sins. He definitely has the authority to do that. May I pray for you?"

"Yes."

I prayed for Crystal and then said, "Now, Crystal, it's your turn to pray. You can ask Jesus to forgive your sins."

She shifted uncomfortably in her chair. "I'll do it later."

"No, now's the time, Crystal. We're here to pray *with* you and support you."

She shifted again. "No, not now."

"Why, Crystal? Why not now? You said you wanted to pray."

"I'm too sleepy."

"Surely you can stay awake for a prayer as important as this."

It was obvious she had become extremely uncomfortable. "I gotta go. I'm really sleepy." Her head began to droop. *What's the deal with this girl?* I began to wonder. *How could she be so awake one minute and practically unconscious the next?*

"Hey, c'mon, Crystal. I'm not here to play games with you. You said you wanted to pray, and we want to pray *with* you."

No response. Her head was still bent toward her chest.

"Crystal? Let me ask you something. What have you been involved in the past few weeks—the past month?"

"I had an abortion," she said groggily. "And I've been messing around with witchcraft."

Now I began putting the pieces together. Satan was the one who was making Crystal too sleepy to pray. The youth leaders and I circled our chairs tightly around her and began praying.

"Satan, you have no authority over this girl. Jesus wants her. You've lost the battle."

In one quick motion, Crystal's head popped to attention, and her eyes...were they glaring *at* me, or were they glaring *through* me? I couldn't tell, but before I had a chance to react, a deep, guttural voice hissed at me: "SSSSShe'ssssss mine, Ssssssusssie!"

Crystal knocked my Bible out of my hand and lunged forward. It took four adult men to hold her in the chair. She was empowered by the father of lies.

"No, she's NOT yours! She wants Jesus. And He's in control now," I screamed.

Crystal calmed down and said, "What happened?" We quickly explained Satan had possession of her and was keeping her from praying.

"Crystal, right now while you have your senses, you need to say you want Jesus!"

"I want..."

Fire in her eyes. The voice was back. "No! She belongs to me!"

Crystal again. "I don't understand what's happening."

"You've allowed Satan into your life, Crystal. By involving yourself with witchcraft and the sin of abortion, you've allowed him to have control. There's a battle going on! It's spiritual warfare right now for your very soul."

"How do I look?" she said.

Seriously? By this time we were into the wee hours of the morning. *We've been sweating, praying, seeking, singing, pleading Christ's blood, and she's worried about her looks?*

"I need a mirror."

"No, Crystal. You need Jesus."

"But my hair—"

"In the name of Jesus Christ, in His blood that was shed for Crystal, and in His authority, I demand to know with whom I'm speaking."

Those glaring, burning, evil eyes again. The stare. Hideous laughter. "I'm Jezebel."

Of course. Now it makes sense. Jezebel—the most wicked woman in the Old Testament. Vain. Prideful. I flipped through the pages in my Bible until I came to 2 Kings 9:30-36 (The Living Bible):

"When Jezebel heard that Jehu had come to Jezreel, she painted her eyelids and fixed her hair and sat at a window. When Jehu entered the gate of the palace, she shouted at him, 'How are you today, you murderer! You son of a Zimri who murdered his master!'

"He looked up and saw her at the window and shouted, 'Throw her down!' So they threw her out the window, and her blood spattered against the wall and on the horses; and she was trampled by the horses' hooves.

"...He told Elijah the prophet that dogs would eat her flesh and that her body would be scattered like manure upon the field, so that no one could tell whose it was."

"Did you hear that, Jezebel? Dogs ate your flesh! We know you're the same demon that inhabited the woman from the Old Testament, and you're a loser! You're vain. Crystal isn't yours. Christ paid too high a price for her. He's not going to let you have her!"

Crystal again, "I want Jesus."

"In the name of Jesus Christ and in His authority, we command Jezebel to leave Crystal at once!"

Crystal leaned forward and yelled and then calmed down. The demon was gone.

"Now, ask Jesus to forgive your sins, Crystal."

Another demon began speaking.

I couldn't believe it. *What?! Jezebel is gone, but there are more?*

Hours passed. Finally around 6 a.m., after several demons had been cast out of Crystal, she asked Christ to forgive her sins and gave Him complete authority of her life.

An entire night had passed. I was drained. But I've never been more sure of Christ's authority than I was in those hours. No question about it: His authority is real.

I was amazed by the display of His wonderful authority. I personally witnessed the battle of good vs. evil, and I saw victory. Christ's authority prevails!

"And they were astonished at His teaching, for He taught them as one having authority, and not as the scribes"
(Mark 1:22 NKJV).

They were **astonished**...that's the word Mark uses. And it's not a light word. In the Greek: *ekpl◆ssō.* Let's look at the meaning: "Thrown off the original course; to cause to be filled with amazement to the point of being overwhelmed, astounded."

They were *thrown off their original course* by His teaching.

Amazed, astounded, overwhelmed by His teaching.

Take a Deep Breath

Let's stop for a minute.

Don't you long for that astonishment?

When was the last time you attended a worship service and were *thrown off your original course?*

How long has it been since you've been amazed by Jesus? Astounded? Overwhelmed? Jaw on the ground saying, "What in the world did I just see?"

That's how they were this day. Why? Remember:

"...for He taught them as one having authority, and not as the scribes"
(Mark 1:22 NKJV).

Let's look at this phrase, break it down, and build a foundation for what's about to occur.

". . . not as the scribes."

What comes to your mind when you hear the title "scribe"? Perhaps you're automatically transported in your mind to a damp cellar. It has a dirt floor, walls of stone and wet with the moisture seeping in from the earth surrounding its foundation.

In the corner is a flickering light of the dancing flame of a half-burned candle. The candle sits upon an old, rickety, wooden desk. As the wax slowly drips over the candelabra you notice motion. There's activity. Something's happening.

Standing hunched over the desk you see a man. He's wearing a burlap robe drawn around his waste by a piece of rope. In his hand is a quill flipping back and forth as he writes ever so carefully. He stops, dips the quill in ink and hurries back to work.

What's he doing?

On the table before him you see a dusty, aged book. The pages are so delicate that you can't help but wonder if they're fragile. You look closer and notice the language written on the old papyrus is unrecognizable. But after a few moments of observation, you realize what's happening. The man is writing. He's translating the text into the language of the day. This man is a scribe!

The man is writing. He's translating the text into the language of the day.

Or perhaps when you hear the term "scribe," you picture a court of law. Seated behind the large wooden desk is a man robed in black, holding a gavel. To his left is a stand occupied by a witness. Two desks hold the books, briefcases, water pitcher, and glasses of battling attorneys.

Words are hurled from left to right, forward and back. All the while, an individual sits to the side pushing the buttons of a tiny machine recording every word.

Who is this incognito typist? The court stenographer. A modern day scribe.

What were scribes like in Jesus' day? Was it someone who stood hunched over a desk translating? Or was a scribe someone who sat hour after hour taking dictation or recording the proceedings of a trial?

You may be relieved to know those aren't accurate descriptions of scribes during Bible times. The scribes were the authoritative instructors of the Law. In today's terms? These were the guys who had gone to seminary. Not only had they earned their undergrad, but they also achieved much more. They'd read all the big books, and they'd no doubt written a few big books of their own.

Reputation

They were entrusted with the Law. They were considered to be a class of scholars who would teach, copy and interpret Jewish law for the people. That's an honorable task, a high position!

These were the lawyers.

Debating is wired into their psyche.

They're the intellectuals.

They're proclaimers of the law.

Protectors of the law.

Prosecutors of the law.

Protectors of the people by the law.

Get the picture?

If not, maybe this will help. They even dressed in a way that the people would realize who they were. They wore special robes. They demanded certain titles. They even expected others to bow in their presence to show the proper respect and regard for their position. In other words: The scribes were somebodies! Well, at least they believed they were.

Remember, they were entrusted with the Law; instructions for God's people from God Himself. But here's the problem: Alongside the Law of God, the scribes began to develop the oral tradition. They were mostly an oral society. That's how things got passed along.

The oral tradition was the interpretation of God's Law by man. In other words, man's opinion of what the Word of God said and how it should be applied to one's life started to become "God's Law."

The more these scribes interpreted the Law, the longer the oral tradition became. And over time they even began to stress man's interpretation over God's instruction, God's law. There's the problem. That's one reason why Sabbath had become anything *but* rest. They had the cease and desist down to the extreme. Minus the rest.

There's always a danger in simply relying on man's opinion. There is no power in man's word, it's all found in *His* Word. Man's instruction is fine in proper perspective. And yet, it can never and *will* never supersede God's Word.

But this is what was happening. The scribes persuaded the people to rely on their word instead of His Word. Therefore, synagogue life had become routine, ordinary, powerless. To say the least, it was less than awe-inspiring.

God's Word in the Flesh

Today, Jesus was in the house!

This Sabbath the people will receive something they weren't expecting.

The source of Authority has shown up.

Today, they will hear from the Master Artist.

When Jesus began to teach, it wasn't the opinion of man. No, it was the very word of God spoken through a man sourced by His Father being proclaimed to the people! Other teachers would stress what Dr. So-and-So would say; Jesus would cite no sources.

He was the Source!

He knew what He was talking about! It flowed through Him.

Wow.

Amazing.

Overwhelming.

Astounding.

They were *thrown off their original course.*

The Source of authority had come to the synagogue!

Well, you can be sure that whenever authority is presented, there will always be confrontation. It's natural—especially in the spiritual realm. Think about it: Light chases away darkness. The two do not go together. Just as oil and water will not mix, darkness is the absence of light. When light shines, darkness flees. It's the same here today.

"Now there was a man in their synagogue with an unclean spirit. And he cried out, saying, 'Let us alone! What have we to do with You, Jesus of Nazareth? Did You come to destroy us? I know who You are—the Holy One of God!'" (Mark 1:23-24 NKJV)

The Light is shining so darkness will be exposed. Inside the synagogue this very same Sabbath is a man "with an unclean spirit." *"With an unclean spirit."*

Let's stop on this phrase for a second. Does the use of the preposition *(with)* give you the thought of a temporary situation? For example, you go the restaurant *with* your friend. You have a nice time together, but that time comes to an end. You might spend a few hours together, but eventually your friend goes one way, and you go yours.

That's not what's happening here.

In this passage *with* is more of a state of being; an issue of control. So it might be better to understand it as being *"in"* an unclean spirit.

See, this evil in his life had totally consumed him. It had taken over his inner being. It controlled his way of thinking. The evil had stolen his life, his person, his identity. At one time he may have been a kind, gentle man. Not anymore. The evil took complete control.

Perhaps he used to be the life of the party—everyone's friend. Forget that. People can't stand to be around him now. In fact, he can't stand himself. He is unequivocally consumed by the evil in his life. His life is beyond his control—evil now controls all he is...his personality, his behavior, his thinking, his actions and reactions. All evil.

Repugnant Vs. Holy

He was in the synagogue this day. What? How can that be? How long has this been going on? Was he a regular attendee? This is the gathering place of God's people, so how could evil feel relaxed where praises were lifted?

Why would the enemy feel comfortable where God's Word was read? Why has this man's lifestyle never been confronted, challenged or changed? It only proves the point: Man's word has no power. The power is found in God's Word alone.

Today, the Source of Authority is in the house. Today the man will be made uncomfortable. This very hour he will have to be dealt with. Now, the confrontation occurs:

"Let us alone! What have we to do with You, Jesus of Nazareth? Did You come to destroy us? I know who You are—the Holy One of God!"'
(Mark 1:24 NKJV)

Here we see a direct confrontation:

Good and evil.

Right and wrong.

Can you imagine the surprise of the evil spirit that day? He thought it was just another ordinary, powerless day. He assumed he would dwell amongst the death and despair within the synagogue that had been created in the religious system of the hour.

Had the evil known Jesus would have been there, he would have never shown up. He would have stayed in the dark. But now that Light has arrived, he's revealed. He's confronted and he's battling for control.

It's interesting…the tactics that evil uses. He recognizes his position and realizes that both he and Jesus can't exist in the same place. Implored is an old sorcerer's tactic: Reveal your enemy, name and position or title, and you have the upper hand. You are in control.

When you hear evil utter the name and title of the Son, don't for an instant believe it's worship. It's a battle. He's revealing himself. Trying to gain the upper hand. It's the challenge for control, a challenge of authority.

Jesus is not afraid of a confrontation. He will not cower from a challenge. In fact, knowing Jesus, this is exactly why He came to this synagogue on this day.

He doesn't back down, nor does He shy away. We don't even find He wants to have a conversation with the disgusting evil that has overtaken this man's life. Instead we hear Him as He speaks:

"Be quiet"
(Mark 1:25 NKJV).

Hold on.

Wait a minute.

Is that what you were expecting? Is there something better to say? "Be quiet…" That's it? If we were in a confrontation with someone trying to control us, and we told him to be quiet, he'd probably laugh. Maybe, he'd even punch us in the mouth. Seriously, that's all? "Be quiet"?

Splash Forward

Again, let's pause for a moment.

Let's look a little deeper into what the original language means. It's probably best illustrated by drawing on an event that hasn't yet occurred in Mark's gospel: Mark 4:35-39.

Briefly, Jesus had been teaching. The disciples had been there with the multitudes. Long day, demanding crowds, so Jesus and the disciples take off in a boat to retreat and rest.

The disciples lounge around the boat while Jesus finds a cushion and falls asleep.

That's enough! The disciples have had all they can take.

As the sun sets, the wind picks up, and the thunder rolls. The boat is tossed—thrown violently—to and fro. Water rushes over the sides. No reason to panic. Remember four of these men are professional fishermen; they've fought the sea before. They're determined not to go down.

While it's true the other disciples may not have been as sea-worthy or skilled in the art of sailing, they knew that water belonged outside the boat. Some are rowing, others holding the sails and the rest scooping.

And Jesus?

He's in the stern, on a cushion, sleeping soundly.

That's enough! The disciples have had all they can take. We hear them as they begin to cry out. "Jesus, we're in a storm. We're doing everything we know to do, but it's not enough! Don't you care?! The boat is filling. Hey Jesus, WE'RE DYING! Help!"

Jesus' response? Well, He doesn't rebuke the disciples at first. Instead, He stands to His feet, walks to the front of the ship, looks the tempest in the eye and speaks. In fact, He uses the same word here as He does in our story today.

"Peace. Be still."

What? That's not any better than, "Be Quiet!"

But, look closely: Be quiet. Peace. Be Still. These are both translated from the Greek term *phimóō*, which means: be muzzled or to deprive of an argument.

Not so wimpy, huh?

Jesus looks the tempest in the eye and says, "Be muzzled!" And suddenly—as suddenly as the storm begins to blow—the hand of God reaches down and grips the mouth of that storm and it can blow no more. You see, when Authority speaks, it must be obeyed.

Come back to our story today.

"Be quiet" (Mark 1:25 NKJV).

There's a confrontation, a challenge for control. The evil that has taken over the identity of this man in the synagogue wants to keep him under its control. The evil spirit recognizes the Source of Authority and tries to get the upper hand.

Jesus will not back down. He speaks: "Be muzzled!" All of a sudden the evil is deprived of its argument.

There. Is. Nothing. More. That. Can. Be. Said.

Authority has spoken, and when authority speaks it must be obeyed. The hand of God reaches down and grips the mouth of this rabid beast. It can speak no more! It has already said too much for too long.

Notice: Jesus doesn't stop there. He never does just enough. He always goes the extra mile. He's an extravagant Savior.

> *"Be quiet, and come out of him!"*
> *(Mark 1:25 NKJV)*

Not only will the evil in this man's life be muzzled. It will be completely removed. See, that's the thing about Jesus. He doesn't only want to silence the evil, He wants to remove it. In other words, He wants to change this man. He wants to renew his identity. He loves him too much to leave him this way. Jesus desires complete restoration for him. Remember the invitation from chapter three of this book (found in Mark 1:16-20)?

Detach from your own way of living life and attach to Him. He's issuing an invitation to walk with Him and become part of Him.

Our part: Respond.

His part: Transform.

> *"And when the unclean spirit had convulsed him and cried out*
> *with a loud voice, he came out of him"*
> *(Mark 1:26 NKJV).*

Kicking and screaming, evil is removed. Remember, when authority speaks, authority must be obeyed.

Cease.

Desist.

Rest.

New Life = Real Sabbath

Can you imagine the relief this man experienced? He was now able to find his identity in Jesus instead of the evil that controlled him for so long.

Now he can finally feel the release and freedom to be who He was intended to be—a masterpiece designed by the Master Artist. It's such an incredible story. Think about it: If Jesus can speak authority over the evil that consumed that man's life, what can He do about the evil that seems to consume you? If Jesus can restore that man's identity, what can He do with yours?

The story's not over.

Remember, Sabbath in the synagogue: A gathering place for God's people. They were there. They saw. And, they were amazed. Today was anything, but average, routine, mundane.

They were *thrown off their original course.*

They worshiped: "We've never seen anything like this!"

"And immediately His fame spread throughout all the region around Galilee"
(Mark 1:28 NKJV).

Could it be that this is what Sabbath was all about? A man reclaimed and people amazed at what Authority had done.

Cease.

Desist.

Rest.

Worship.

That was the plan from the beginning.

That's Sabbath.

Yes, it's about worship. Sure, it's about giving praise to the only One who deserves it. But it's also about *you.* Taking the time you need to rearrange priorities, shift your thinking, cease your working. A time to refuel. An opportunity to be empowered. Time to re-examine your relationship with Him. Enjoying who you are in Him—a prize!

Yes, that's Sabbath.

And it's integral in becoming the masterpiece the Artist created you to be.

Going Deeper

(To be answered individually or with a small group.)

• Have you built a Sabbath into your weekly routine? Do you make yourself have a genuine day of rest? Have you learned to cease, desist, rest, and truly worship? Or is your Sabbath merely a two-hour church service?

• Can you describe a time in your life when you were *thrown off course* by God's teaching?

• Have you seen Him show off? Have you been amazed by Him?

• What kind of authority have you allowed Christ to have in your life?

• Mark clearly shows us in his Gospel account that Christ IS the Authority over evil. Is there anything in your life you need His authority to overcome?

• What would your life look like if Christ's authority consumed you, energized you, saturated you, lived *through* you?

Prayer time: Make a list of the things this chapter has prompted you to pray about and start praying.

CHAPTER
FIVE

God is the Master.

He created all.

There is none above His supremacy.

The universe and everything in it have to succumb to His voice.

He is absolute authority.

The Master Artist is at work.

When He paints, He paints with urgency and beauty.

AT ONCE

(Luke 4:38-41; Mark 1:29-31)

"What in the world have we seen?"

"What is this?"

That's what they were saying. At least all those who had been in the synagogue that day. On just another Sabbath at just another Sabbath gathering, the Master Artist—the source of Authority had shown up.

He had authority over the realm of truth: He taught as if He knew what He was talking about. He spoke differently; there was a knowledge, a passion; not as the scribes.

He had authority over the spiritual realm: He muzzled and removed the evil from one man's life.

He muzzled and removed the evil from one man's life.

They had been thrown off their original course. They were amazed. In a very public way, Jesus began to reveal His identity by His authority. Truly, He was the source. It had been displayed at the gathering place for the Jewish people. It was a big deal. And the day wasn't over.

"Now, as soon as they had come out of the synagogue…"
(Mark 1:29 NKJV).

Urgency

We get the sense from words like "immediately," "as soon as," "straightway," "then," "now," "at once," that we're on a journey that just can't be delayed. Keep up! You can't slow down. You might miss something. The Artist is painting with urgency.

With the opening phrase of verse 29 *"Now, as soon as they*

had come out of the synagogue," we're going to transition from a very public event to an extremely private location. We're traveling from the synagogue to a home. Be sure, this is not just any home.

> *"...they entered the house of Simon and Andrew, with James and John"*
> *(Mark 1:29 NKJV).*

It's the family home of the fishermen. This would become an important location to Jesus and His ministry in this region of Capernaum. It seems this home would become His headquarters — where He sets up shop.

Can you imagine what could have been going through their minds? They had been in the synagogue that day. They had seen authority displayed. How excited they must have been.

As we walk through the front door with these men, we discover another story. We meet a new character in the drama. We see a new face on the canvas. She's an important woman to Simon and his family.

> *"But Simon's wife's mother..."*
> *(Mark 1:30 NKJV).*

Isn't the power of a conjunction amazing? You know — those words that have the ability to change everything. A picture filled with beauty and style is being painted. All of a sudden you hit a conjunction (but, however, although), and you know the entire scene can change depending on what follows.

This is because conjunctions are connecting words and everything hangs on what they're connected to.

"...lay sick with a fever..."
(Mark 1:30 NKJV).

*The air has left
the room.*

In just one statement we transition from one extreme to another. We go from the excitement of the synagogue to the despair of Simon's home. In this *moment* we're brought down from the cloud we've been floating on, because now we see real need. The air has left the room. We see this woman in a desperate situation.

With a fever... Do you remember the man we met back in the synagogue who was with an evil spirit? If so, you'll remember the discussion we had about the idea of being "with."

Remember, this is referring more to a state of being rather than a temporal condition. She is consumed by this fever. She didn't simply wake up this morning and feel a cold coming on. It's not that her temperature is a little high.

No. She was victimized by her condition; consumed. So consumed, that Luke refers to her condition as a "great fever" in Luke 4:38.

Massive Illness

It's evidenced by the tense of the word.

"Lay sick" in the Greek language is in the imperfect tense. And the imperfect tense is that tense in the Greek language that refers to a *continued action.*

Or, technically speaking, it's the verb tense where the writer portrays an action in process, or a state of being that is occurring in the past with no assessment of the action's completion.[1]

In today's language: Her sickness has *been* happening and is *still* happening.

She's consumed.

She's overcome.

Life is literally being drained from her body.

So much so that we see she's confined to her bed. The ability to move around the house has been yanked from her. She has fallen victim to this condition. It was about to claim what little of her life remained.

She was desperate.

So were Simon and Andrew.

They had been in the synagogue. They had witnessed the very public display of their Teacher's authority. And, seeing how He had given the demon-possessed man his life back, they believed He could meet their need as well.

> *"...they told Him about her at once"*
> *(Mark 1:30 NKJV).*

They waste no time. They take action! As soon as they cross the threshold of the home, they tell Jesus about this woman *at once*. We sense the urgency in these two words.

Promptly.

Instantly.

Immediately.

They took initiative. They didn't wait. Something had to be done. The One who was able to do something was there. Now. He had the ability, the power to move in their circumstance. They saw. They

1   Heiser, M. S. (2005).*Glossary of Morpho-Syntactic Database Terminology*. Logos Bible Software.

believed. They reacted to that belief. They told Him about her. *At once.*

What Would He Do?

Now, watch what happens…

"So He came…"
(Mark 1:31 NKJV).

Jesus responds to their need. When He hears about the woman's condition we watch as He goes to where she is. There's something beautiful in that. This is the story that's repeated over and again. Jesus always goes.

He goes to John.

He goes to the Jordan.

He goes to the fishermen.

He goes to the synagogue.

He goes to the woman.

He goes to you.

He goes to me.

It's the constant pursuit of the Master Artist longing to complete His masterpiece.

Simon didn't yell up the stairs: "Hey, Mom! Get down here. Jesus wants you."

It's not even the woman in her feeble condition, dragging herself to His feet. Simon and Andrew didn't each get under her arms and carry her to Jesus.

He pursues. He goes to her. Then the action continues.

"…and took her by the hand…"
(Mark 1:31 NKJV).

Jesus enters the room where she's confined. No doubt, it's all about her. He gives this woman His undivided attention. He looks at her while she's struggling through this condition. He sees her. He knows her need. Then He reaches down to where she is and takes her by the hand.

Her strength is gone. Her condition is severe. She can't make her way to Jesus. He comes to her. Jesus reaches down and takes her by the hand.

"...lifted her up..."
(Mark 1:31 NKJV).

He refuses to leave her confined in bed. He will not leave her to struggle alone. That's the way Jesus is: He always pursues, comes to where we are, but refuses to leave us there. We are a work in progress; He always has something more in mind. He sees the beautiful creation we can become with His touch.

He will not leave her to struggle alone.

From Susie:

I used to teach high school speech, drama, English, and creative writing. Zach was failing speech class simply because he refused to give any of his speeches. I liked Zach and really wanted him to pass. I tried to encourage him. I wanted him to succeed. I thought he had potential and could land a part in one of our drama productions if he could just gain confidence from giving a speech first.

Zach sat in the back of the room and usually responded with a grunt when spoken to.

"Do you have your speech outline?" I asked.

"No," he grunted.

We listened to a few more speeches, and at the end of class, Zach approached my desk. "Miss Shellenberger," he grunted. "I know what I'm gonna do my speech on."

I was thrilled! "Zach, this is great! I'm so happy you're rising to the occasion. I just know you'll do a good job."

"Uh, yeah." He handed me a piece of notebook paper with his outline on it. "I'm gonna do a speech," he said, "on how to set a house on fire."

"Excuse me?" I said. "A speech on how to set a house on fire? Zach, you know these are informative speeches with the requirement to demonstrate as you speak."

"Uh, yeah."

I nervously cleared my throat. "Uh, Zach, how will you, uh... demonstrate this?"

His eyes lit up with an eerie glow. "I'm gonna make me a house, and I'm gonna bring it in here and put it on top of your desk and soak it in gasoline, and I'm gonna set it on fire."

I was so happy he'd finally come up with an idea and was willing to participate! I didn't want to take the excitement away from him by saying, "Are you kidding? We can't have a FIRE in the classroom! This is a public school!"

But I didn't want to over-encourage him either with, "Well, hot dog, Zach! We'll gather 'round and make s'mores, too!"

So I simply told him I'd need to seek permission about

having a fire in the classroom. I was shocked when the principal said, "Well, you have fire extinguishers. Make sure it's a little house out of Popsicle sticks and just be ready. If it's that small though, I can't imagine anything getting out of control. But just to be sure, have a couple of guys nearby ready to help. I, too, am glad that Zach is trying."

So I gave Zach the news, "OK, Zach. We have permission. But remember, when you make this house out of Popsicle sticks, it has to be really small. Miniscule is the operative word here."

Uh, yeah, uh, got it," he said.

The House

The next day, Zach and half the football team wheeled the "house" in on a dolly then carefully lifted it to my desk. I was sitting in the back of the room—as I usually did when grading speeches—but gasped when I saw this thing. A house? No. This was more like a *home*. A group of Pygmies could have been very happy living inside.

I was in shock. He poured gasoline on top of the house and began his speech. I noticed an eerie glow as he spoke. It was amazing how much this kid knew about fires. I swallowed and wondered if there was any way he knew where I lived.

Zach talked about faulty wiring, electrical shorts, bad outlets, carelessness with electric blankets and candles, and I couldn't help but notice his passion. He really had the scoop! He *knew* his subject, and he was giving it all he had.

At a strategic moment, he reached inside his pocket and pulled out a cigarette lighter and set that home ablaze. Students screamed. We ran. I panicked and was sure I saw a tunnel of light leading me to heaven. But in one fluid motion, Zach grabbed the fire extinguisher, pulled the pin and the fire was gone.

I was speechless. Partly because of the smoke. But also because I was so impressed with Zach. I gave him an A+ on that speech. He deserved it. He gave it all he had, and it was truly amazing.

Zach ended up giving a few more speeches that year and passed the class. The following year, he even signed up for drama. He gained the confidence I thought he would get from speech class. And Zach landed a great role in our all-school production of "Bye Bye Birdie."

A teacher sees the potential in what a student can become.

The Master Artist knows the reality of a masterpiece in the making. Jesus saw past how sick the woman was, and focused instead of what she could do if made whole. It was all about her.

Notice, there's no conversation recorded in this encounter. Only the words immediately spoken by Simon and Andrew when they entered the home. But that's all it took. In response, Jesus goes to where she is, reaches down, takes her by the hand and lifts her up.

> "...immediately the fever left her"
> (Mark 1:31 NKJV).

Did you catch it?

Don't miss the progression: Simon and Andrew tell Jesus about her *at once.*

Jesus goes to where she is.

When He gets to the place she is laying, He reaches down and takes her by the hand.

He lifts her up.

And when He lifts her up, what consumes her stays down.

Promptly.

Instantly.

Immediately.

What medical science could not do, Jesus did.

When there seemed to be no hope, He was there.

When life was about to end, Jesus gave new life.

Jesus changed her state of being.

What *had been happening* and *was happening* was corrected: The fever left her, immediately!

Life restored. Now what?

> "...*And immediately she arose and served them*"
> (*Luke 4:39 NKJV*).

She served them. Continually. How do we know? Again, we go back to the Greek language—the original language in which the New Testament was written. "*And she served them*" is written in the imperfect tense in the Greek. She would serve the One who had lifted her. How could she do any less? He had lifted her to new life; she would spend her life serving Him.

When He lifts her up, what consumes her stays down.

It's Not Over Yet

What an incredible day so far! There was a public display of His authority in the synagogue: A man was restored. People were amazed. Then, there was a private display of His authority: A woman was lifted to new life.

It all happened because they told Him about her, *at once.*
Promptly. Instantly. Immediately.
Then her life was changed.

The Action Continues

"When the sun was setting..."
(Luke 4:40 NKJV).

As soon as the sun goes down, the action begins all over again.
Let's recap the progression of our passage: The day began with a very
public display of His authority in the synagogue, then we transition to
a very private location where we see a private display of His authority
in a home. Now, in an instant, the private location turns into a public
event.

Remember, these folks had been at the synagogue. They had
been thrown from their normal course. They were left with their jaws
on the ground, amazed. Just as Simon and Andrew didn't waste time to
tell Jesus about the struggle going on inside their home, we sense these
people were anxious to bring their needs to Jesus as well.

But because of the "rules" of the Sabbath they had to wait,
otherwise, there would have been a run on
the house before now. To carry a sick person
from one place to another was considered
work. And there was no work allowed on
the Sabbath. See how man's rules muddy
everything when mixed with God's rules?

Man's rules muddy everything when mixed with God's rules.

Again, God created the Sabbath for rest, but He also created it
for man's benefit—not to box him in—but to give him freedom on this

day. But logic was thrown out the window when man got involved with interpreting the rules and demanding they were from God.

When the Sabbath was over—and it was considered over at sundown—they were off to Simon and Andrew's house...all because Jesus was there.

"When the sun was setting, all those who had any that were sick with various diseases brought them to Him; and He laid His hands on every one of them and healed them. And demons also came out of many"
(Luke 4:40-41 NKJV).

Do you see it? Do you understand their longing, their drive? If Jesus was able to change the life of someone consumed with evil, what could He do with a life dedicated to Him? Certainly, if He didn't cower from a confrontation in the synagogue, He'd respond the same here. They had real needs, and they took these needs to Jesus as soon as they were able, according to the law.

Let's Dig a Little Deeper

There even seems to be something more here, doesn't there? It's not just their need. Let's read the verse again: *They brought all who were sick and who were demon possessed.*

Amazing. All.

They brought all.

And kept bringing (again, the imperfect tense in the Greek language, so it means that continued urgency we talked about earlier).

Do you sense they understood Jesus had the answer to every problem? That they believed He was able to meet every need? It seems as if they felt nothing was too big, too impossible. No situation too powerful. He was the Source of Authority. They had seen. They acted.

Wherever they came from, whatever they were dealing with, they believed. They were beginning to understand the Artist would focus on each individual need.

"And the whole city was gathered together at the door..."
(Mark 1:32-33 NKJV).

They were beginning to understand the Artist would focus on each individual need.

What a crowd! This would be any event promoter's dream come true. The whole city was there. These are the gospel writer's words. The entire city gathered together. They brought all—*kept bringing to Jesus*—those who were in need. In other words, no one was left behind. What an extraordinary response, especially considering they're at Simon and Andrew's home!

The stage is set.

What will happen next?

"Then He healed many who were sick with various diseases, and cast out many demons; and He did not allow the demons to speak, because they knew Him"
(Mark 1:34 NKJV).

He displayed Kingdom authority. He restored lives. He met their needs. Let's go back to how Luke puts it:

"...He laid His hands on every one of them and healed them"
(Luke 4:40 NKJV).

Every. One. Of. Them.

Will you take my hand for a moment?

Come with me to the door of Simon and Andrew's home.

It's overwhelming to see the multitude of faces that have gathered here. It's even more staggering when you notice the condition of those who have come.

They're sick.

Life has worked some of them over and beaten many down. There are far too many lines on these faces, and each line tells a tragic story. Do you see the eight-year-old boy who has been atrociously burned? The other children are afraid of him. His little face is a twisted, gnarled mess.

There are far too many lines on these faces, and each line tells a tragic story.

Notice the young mother holding her disfigured baby. She doesn't understand; she assumes it's her fault. She's blaming herself for the birth defects.

And that man over there—he must be close to 100 years old. Pus oozes from his eyes. He can't hear, and you can tell he's in pain by the way he's limping.

And the lepers! They're not even supposed to be here. What—

Then, you see Him.

You see the silhouette of a man walk through the door and down into the crowd. Jesus! He's touching all those in need.

Despair? No longer.

Fear? No more.

Confusion? No way.

And when He touches them…

Promptly. Instantly. Immediately.

They receive exactly what they need.

Life restored. Again and again.

Every. One. Of. Them.

Jesus is no respecter of persons. It didn't matter who they were, what they were dealing with, where they came from: He touched them all. That's Kingdom prerogative. That's Kingdom Authority. That's Jesus. That's the Master Artist at work.

Sundown

Eventually the day comes to an end and we're turning it over in our minds:

Jesus is the Source of Authority. He has authority over the realm of truth. He displayed His authority over the spiritual realm.

Physical realm? Yep, authority there too.

Emotional, relational—He has authority over every realm.

He is the Source of Authority.

I wonder: What's keeping you down?

What's consuming you?

Tell Him *at once.*

He'll come to where you are.

He'll reach down to you.

There's no pit too deep.

He can reach into the cavern of emotional despair.

He's stronger than the bullying arm of addiction.

He's more powerful than any rift of relationship.

He'll reach all the way down to wherever you may be.

He'll lift you up. And, when He does, what consumes you must stay down. Hope reborn. Life renewed.

He'll come to where you are. He'll reach down to you. There's no pit too deep.

Go ahead, tell Him.

At once!

Going Deeper

(To be answered individually or with a small group.)

- You've just left church. What did you see, hear, experience? Was the Word preached with Christ's authority? Did the praise and worship point attention to Him? Were you "knocked off your original course"?
- Share a time when you were too weak to ask for God's help, but He came to you and offered complete restoration.
- When you have things you need to talk with Christ about, do you carry them around for a while, or do you go *at once* to Him?
- Why is Christ sometimes the last One to Whom we go?
- How does it make you feel to know He looks past where you are right now, and sees the potential in you? He knows what you can become.
- The Master desires to complete His masterpiece. That's you! What needs to stay down as He lifts you up to become all He dreams for you?

Prayer time: Oh, Father, thank You that You see and know everything! I don't want to stay where I am spiritually; I want to be continually moving toward You. I want continued motion in our relationship. Please lift me up and help me let go of all that needs to remain behind. Amen.

CHAPTER
SIX

A freak.

That's what he was.

Friendless and untouchable.

A leper living a death sentence.

Have you ever felt like this?

No matter what you do, it won't be good enough?

You'll always be on a downward spiral?

Where do you go when you're broken, unwanted and ostracized?

You go to the One with open arms of healing, love and restoration.

COMPLETE MAKEOVER
(Mark 1:35-42)

Jesus is on the move.

The Kingdom's going public. He's unveiling the canvas, and you're on it.

It's why He came.

He's into complete restoration.

> *"Now a piece of human garbage came to Him"*
> *(Mark 1:40 NKJV).*

Human garbage.

A piece of walking human garbage approached Him.

No. Scripture doesn't say that. But it could have, because that's exactly how lepers were viewed: human trash. No value. Lower than dogs.

Here's what Scripture really says:

> *"Now a leper came to Him..."*
> *(Mark 1:40 NKJV).*

In the midst of the excitement of the Kingdom being proclaimed, we meet him. It's the most unlikely visitor anyone would expect.
A leper.

Lepers were forced loners. They couldn't touch, nor be touched. To be pronounced a leper was to be given a death sentence.

Imagine. You've been to the doctor. Tests have been run. The phone rings. Your results are back. Bad news. You have leprosy.

No. This can't be true, you think.

I have a wedding to plan.

I'm going on a missions' trip.

Our family vacation is already on the calendar.

Tickets for the cruise have been purchased.

Not for you.

You're a leper.

You're now living with a death sentence.

Not only will you become more and more physically ill, but now you're an outcast. You can say goodbye to your family, but there's no time to tell your friends. Take a good look at your home; you'll never see it again. You're banished to an off-limits area outside the city limits. It's a small leper colony filled with others—like you—who also have the disease.

It reeks with the smell of rotting flesh.

It's a garbage dump filled with human trash.

Vultures dive low and pick pieces of diseased flesh off the bones of the infected.

No one clean is here. No outsider ever visits.

Laughter is absent. Friendships don't exist.

This. Is. Now. Your. Life.

Hell on earth.

That's what a leper colony was like.

What *Is* Leprosy?

Leprosy is still a horrible disease, but in North America we don't hear much about it, because we have it under control. It's now called Hansen's disease, and about 95 percent of the population has a natural immunity to it. It's extremely treatable if found in time.

Contrary to what you may think, it's not as though a leper's foot would suddenly drop off. It's a progressive bacterial disease. If the infection began in the foot, the nerve endings would be affected. So the victim may walk across a burning coal or get a nail stuck in his foot and not even feel it because of the damaged nerves and his inability to know pain.

So he keeps walking on the damaged foot, and eventually the infection spreads and the victim will lose his foot—and other extremities—if not treated.

The Old Testament gives very clear instruction for the people of biblical times who became infected. If you noticed a rash, spot, sore, or deformity upon your flesh that wasn't supposed to be there, you were required by law to present yourself to the priest. He'd be the examiner—though he wouldn't be trained in the medical sciences.

He'd have some guidelines: If it looked like this, if it's shaped like that, if it's this color, if it has hair coming out of it, or if it smells this way. (Check out Leviticus 13.) By this, he'd determine what the rash, spot, sore, or deformity was. If it didn't fit into one of the categories, the individual would be secluded for a certain period of time, to wait and pray that it would get better or go away. If it didn't, their lives would never be the same.

"Unclean!"

This would become their cry. Forsaken and ostracized. The disease was far too contagious to take any chances, and the Law made it very clear:

> "He is unclean, and he shall dwell alone"
> (Leviticus 13:46).

We were not made to dwell alone. We need people. Family. Friends. Companionship. In fact, search Scripture and you'll find the first thing God pronounces as 'not good' is that man should not be alone (Genesis 2:18). Everybody needs community: a listening ear, shared laughter, and a shoulder to cry on. But now, because of his condition: alone.

> *"…his dwelling shall be outside the camp"*
> *(Leviticus 13:46).*

From Billy:

I'll never forget the kindness of Pastor Jerry Knouse of the Church of the Open Door in Richfield, Pa. I was preaching special services in his church. He treated me with such kindness as I shared with him the importance of needing to leave early. It was due to the news I just received from my wife telling me she didn't want me to come home. He did everything he could to get me on the road quickly. I saw Jesus in him that early morning in December.

As I pulled out of the gravel parking lot, so many things were going through my mind. I remember seeing the church in my rearview mirror as I pulled away; daylight was breaking on this winter morning and it was such a beautiful sight. One I will never forget.

A new day was dawning; life would go on.

I just didn't know what that life would look like for me.

It was the longest eight hours I have ever spent on the road. Questions raced through my mind. Thoughts bombarded me from left to right. I was consumed with the situation. I was hurt. I was confused. I felt guilty. I felt shame. I was angry. I'm a fixer, but I couldn't fix this.

So Many Questions

I needed to talk to someone. But whom do you call when your world is crumbling? How do you admit you're a failure, that you've failed in your relationship with your wife? Where do you seek advice?

I know a lot of people. It's just the nature of what I do. I'm in a different place every week with a different group of people. I know a lot of folks. But I have very few close friends. The one I thought of first? Brian. I could call him. He would never judge me. He would listen, be honest and give me good advice.

So I called him. Brian was there for me in that dark hour. I'll forever be appreciative for his love and godly advice. It calmed my spirit and settled my thoughts. At least a little.

I made it to Cincinnati and went to my mother's house. I figured my wife needed some space. I wanted to respect that.

Minutes ticked off the clock. Hours dragged by. Days drudged on. Weeks crawled past. Yet, there seemed to be no change. My wife and I would talk. We would argue. We would cry. We'd even have dinner. But we couldn't get to where we needed to be.

I had to make a decision. Should I resume my speaking schedule, or stay home? I did what I thought was right. I cancelled my spring and summer schedule for that year. I would stay in Cincinnati and work on my relationship. It was the right decision.

Changes

If I were going to stay home, I would need a job. That was an interesting dilemma. What would I do? What *could* I do? My educational training was in religion. I had been a youth pastor early in my ministry and had been traveling as an evangelist since 1998. It was now 2006. I was 33 years old. I wondered if I were qualified to do anything else.

Then, besides the job, where would I attend church? This was a struggle for me. You have to understand: I couldn't slip into services incognito. People would know who I was. This was my home. They would notice my wife wasn't with me. They would have heard the rumors (my phone was ringing off the hook). How do you face those things?

So, I didn't.

I thought I could make it on my own.

I would handle it. I couldn't take that step. I wasn't ready. (I know, looking back, this doesn't make sense. If anybody should have known this was the exact time I needed the church, it should have been me. It's a story I've seen played over and again. When trouble comes, people stay away. I'm embarrassed now for that to be my response. But it was.)

The job situation worked out. I was employed by a local Toyota dealership. It wasn't the idea position, but it was a good one. I was now officially a new car salesman. In the matter of a month I had gone from being on top of the world preaching Jesus—to pushing vehicles. I went from living on the road to living in a car dealership. And I kept asking myself over and over: *Is this what my life has become?*

Turnaround

There's so much more that could be told in this story. But here's where I ended up finding myself. Despite everything, my marriage was never reconciled. I never returned to my home. I felt my ministry was gone.

That was until June of that year. I went to a camp meeting service where a good friend of mine was preaching. I arrived late and planned to leave early to avoid any awkward meetings or questions. I still remember the anxiety of going.

My friend, David, was preaching that evening from Psalm 63:1, "God, You are my God," and I have no doubt, it was for me. God orchestrated this meeting.

As I listened to the story of King David running from a son who wanted him dead, dwelling in the desert away from the palace, having lost it all; I was amazed he was still able to say (and I'm paraphrasing): "Everything You are God, is everything I need. You are exactly what I need—exactly when I need it. You are MY God!"

Why had I waited? Why had I struggled?

He had the answer. He *was* the answer. Everything I needed. Exactly *what* I needed.

Next thing you know, I was kneeling at an altar pouring out my hurt, my fear, my confusion, to a God who had been waiting the past six months to meet with me. In that instant, a weight was lifted from my shoulders. I heard His affirming voice, as my friend David spoke these words to me: "Billy, God's not finished with you. He has great plans for your life. Believe that. Trust Him. It's not over."

And boy was he telling the truth!

(There's more to the story, but I'll share it a little later.)

Where do you go when you're unwanted? When you're the outcast?

Who do you turn to when your world is in turmoil? Disrepair?

Who do you speak to when no one wants to listen?

Compassion Recognized

Today, a leper comes to Jesus.

With nowhere else to turn. Nowhere else to go. This broken creation makes his way to the Master Artist.

Have you ever noticed that wherever you find Jesus, you usually find crowds of people? Except for those solitary times of prayer there are always crowds of people, and usually at least 12 guys somewhere in the shadows.

Many times we see hundreds. Sometimes there are even thousands. There's something about Jesus that draws a crowd. Today would be no different. Jesus has been advancing the Kingdom. Matthew puts this event in chapter eight, right after the Sermon on the Mount.

This broken creation makes his way to the Master Artist.

So the multitude is there. They've been listening to Jesus preach with authority.

Do you see it?

Jesus is *surrounded* by the multitude.

Everyone seems to be captivated by His presence. That is, everybody except for the group of people toward the back. They're whispering, pointing. What's the distraction?

You're there. You're part of the crowd. Go ahead. Turn around and see what's happening.

Looking in the direction where one is pointing, you see him.

He's hobbling toward the crowd—toward you. You can't help but notice his unkempt hair, torn clothing and covered face.

Gasp!

It's a leper.

"Hey! What's he doing here?"

"Someone lasso the trash and drag him back to where he belongs!"

You notice those around you covering their noses, and you smell it, too: the odor of decaying flesh. The stench of rotting skin is unmistakable. Several begin to gag.

But the leper continues. He's not looking at the crowd.

He's focused on an audience of One.

The people know if they breathe the same air, touch the same ground, they, too, will be defiled. So they back away.

But look! As the multitude parts, Jesus stands firmly in place, unwavering. Undaunted. Unafraid.

This leper continues toward Jesus with his head cast down, ashamed of his condition and fearing for his life. Watching from a distance, you see him fall on his face before Jesus.

Listen to his trembling voice. What's he saying?

We listen as he begins to worship at His feet. We hear him as he begins to speak. Listen to his trembling voice. What's he saying?

Compassion Requested

> *"If You are willing, You can make me clean"*
> *(Mark 1:40 NKJV).*

Notice, he's not saying, "If You're able." In fact, there's no question of ability in that statement. He obviously believes Jesus has the ability and the authority to restore his life.

In the context of this day, the people would have believed the following: *He's getting from God exactly what he deserves. This is payment—a penalty for his sin. God removed His hand of mercy from this pitiful man's life.*

See, that's how the people could justify their lack of compassion. If God didn't love this man, why should they? But, the leper believes if Jesus is the Promised One—the One who acts on God's behalf—then He could, should He choose, extend His hand of mercy. He could show compassion, and love, and restore his broken life.

Compassion's Response

How would Jesus respond? Keep watching.

> *"Then Jesus, moved with compassion…"*
> *(Mark 1:41 NKJV).*

Can we pause here for a moment? When we read that Jesus is "moved with compassion" we need to know this is really strong language. "Moved with compassion" in the Greek language is *splanchnizomai*. It's pronounced: *Splangkh-nid'-zom-ahee*. And it means: *to be moved as to one's bowels; to feel deep sympathy for; to be moved with compassion.* The bowels were thought to be the hub of love and pity.

It's referring to a deep inner emotion that's generated from the seat of passions. It's an arousal of emotion that results in response. This is coming from the place where anger is born, where frustration exists or indignation is found. But, it's also the birthplace of tender affections such as love and care. Jesus is moved by a feeling of deep sympathy and sorrow, so much so that it's accompanied by the strong desire to alleviate suffering.

In other words, **it broke His heart.**

He saw the isolation. He recognized the hurt, the pain.

Jesus was moved by the leper's condition.

This strong phrase ("moved with compassion") is used almost exclusively in Scripture to describe what happens inside Jesus. At least eight times in the Gospels we run across this phrase. We see it four times in Matthew, three times in Mark and twice in Luke. It's referring to what's going on inside of Him.

> *It broke His heart.*
> *He saw the isolation.*
> *He recognized the*
> *hurt, the pain.*

Please.

A leper comes to Jesus. Begging. Pleading: "If You are willing…"

What would Jesus do? With the Father's heart pounding in His chest, He…

". . . stretched out *His* hand and touched him."

Jesus does the unthinkable.

And He does it without hesitation!

He reaches out and touches the unclean. Can you see how far compassion is willing to go?

What others were afraid of, Jesus was not. When all society was willing to throw this man away, Jesus would not. When everyone else turned their backs, Jesus could not.

He touches the untouchable! He reaches down, takes the man by the face so they're looking eye to eye. When he looked into Jesus' face he saw the Father's heart.

> *"…said to him, 'I am willing; be cleansed'"*
> *(Mark 1:41 NKJV).*

I want to.

I am willing.

Be clean.

Compassion's Result

"As soon as He had spoken, immediately the leprosy left him,
and he was cleansed"
(Mark 1:42 NKJV).

Life is restored. Jesus didn't receive what the man had when He touched him. The leper received what Jesus had. Real life. Restoration. The outcast is now part of community. His life is changed.

It was the Father's tender heart pounding in His chest.

It moved Him.

It's what He wanted to do.

It's what He's still doing.

Touching the unclean places of our lives.

Making whole what we've broken and tried to hide.

He places His holy hands onto our tear-stained faces and lifts our eyes to meet His.

And He makes us whole.

This is the Artist.

Restoring His loved masterpiece.

Going Deeper

(To be answered individually or with a small group.)

- The Father is the Source of Compassion, and Jesus reveals the Father's heart. He wants to touch and bring wholeness to the "untouchable" areas of our lives. What would most people say those areas are? (Sin, fear, shame, depression, anger, worry, porn, gossip, etc.)
- What motivates us to be more Christ-like? What's going on in the Father is going on in the Son. What's going on in the Son should be going on in us. We should be His eyes, hands, feet, and heart. Are we willing to touch the untouchables for Jesus?
- We discussed the strong meaning behind the phrase "moved with compassion." It describes what's happening inside Jesus. Read these other places in Scripture where the phrase is also used and discuss the similarity you see Jesus feeling in these verses, and in what Jesus felt for the leper. (Matthew 9:36, 14:14, 15:32, 20:34. Mark 1:41, 6:34, 9:36. Luke 7:13, 15:20)
- What's keeping you "outside the camp"? Is there an area in your life that's causing you to dwell alone when you could be a vital part of the Kingdom community?

Prayer time: Ask Jesus to reveal any "untouchable" areas in your life that are keeping you from intimacy with Him. When He brings an area to your mind, thank Him for showing it to you. Then, with His help, commit that area to Him. Give it to your Master.

CHAPTER
SEVEN

Why is it when we're told "don't touch," we're drawn to touching?

When we're instructed not to cross the line, we put one toe over to simply see what will happen?

It's called sin.

Demanding our own way because of a carnal nature.

How often does disobedience matter? Always.

DISOBEDIENCE COSTS
(Mark 1:43-45)

From Susie:

I had the privilege of meeting Mother Teresa in 1996. I volunteered some time in her "Home of the Destitute and Dying" in Calcutta, and I got to spend a day in one of her leper colonies. It was a fascinating place. These outcasts had become an entire community unto themselves.

They grew their own food, made their own clothing, sustained themselves. Medical staff came and went, and attended to their needs. Of course, most of the lepers looked atrocious. Some looked normal—leprosy had attacked them, but they had not lost any limbs yet, nor had they become deformed.

I'll never forget 14-year-old Nilaya. While other girls her age were concerned about their hair, crushing on boys and completing homework assignments, she was missing a foot. Yes, leprosy had invaded her life. No longer would she share a desk with a friend at school, go to the movies, shop at the market, or browse the library. She was now alone—alone in a crowd of diseased adults. And even though they loved her, nurtured and accepted her, the problem was...*she was now one of them.*

She was a leper.

Amazing.

Incredible.

Exciting.

Choose any positive adjective—they'll all work here! Because there's simply no other way to describe what just happened. In the midst of the Kingdom going public, a leper came to Jesus. And it wasn't just any leper. This was a man who was "full" of the disease according to Luke 5:12.

All that had been lost was now recovered.

That means the *effects* of the disease had taken place:

His flesh was rotting,

limbs were missing,

hair was gone,

and he had the lion's face that comes with Hansen's disease.

The medical term is *leonine facies*—because of the "lion like effects" to the face. The cartilage in the nose dissolves, nerves die, the face sags, and if the ears are still attached, the lobes become thick and lumpy.

And yet, he went where he was unwanted and unwelcome, and he requested healing from Jesus.

Without hesitation, that's exactly what Jesus did. With the Father's heart pounding in His chest, He reaches out and touches the untouchable.

Can you believe it? He touched the leper.

In that touch, the leper was made whole. The crowd is shocked.

They heard Jesus speak of His willingness to heal, and as the syllables flipped off His tongue, this man was transformed before their very eyes.

All that had been lost was now recovered:

rotting flesh = brand-new baby soft skin,

limbs that were gone = regenerated and healthy limbs,

extremities such as an absent nostril, half an ear, missing lips = instant facelift.

They all saw it.

They were all mesmerized.

Understand, the work that Jesus did in that man's life went much deeper than just the physical. Everything the disease had taken from him was now returned.

If he was married, he could now be united with his wife.

If he had children, he could play ball with his boy and tuck his daughter into bed at night

His home was no longer in the leper colony, but back under their roof. He could share their meals, attend synagogue, and once again, experience a connected life with his loved ones.

He received total restoration: physically, spiritually, emotionally, relationally! Completely restored to community.

The story continues:

"And He strictly warned him and sent him away at once"
(Mark 1:43 NKJV).

Can we stop here for a moment? Does this seem odd to you? Jesus has just worked an incredible miracle in this man's life; He has completely restored him in every aspect of restoration and now He's strictly warning him?

This is an interesting word in the original language we translate: "He strictly warned." The term *embrimaomai* (em-brim-ah'-om-ahee) carries with it the meaning of speaking harshly to; to scold, to sternly warn or to snort.

Yes. To snort. It's actually the term used to describe scarcely controlled animal fury. In other words, it means to flare one's nostrils with all the audibles that accompany that activity.

What?!?

Have you ever flared your nostrils? Or, have you ever had someone flare their nostrils at you?

It really brings an interesting picture to mind, doesn't it? It's the bull in the ring scraping the dirt with his hoof as he flares his nostrils preparing to charge.

It's the unbridled stallion in the coral refusing to be broken as he flares his nostrils in defiance.

Can you see it? Jesus flares His nostrils. He snorts at the man! Does your Jesus snort? That's a humorous picture. It's a picture that not only seems out of character, but also out of place.

Jesus has just restored this man! It's the result of compassion. It's the restoration of a masterpiece. Then? He snorts and thrusts him away, saying:

"See that you say nothing to anyone"
(Mark 1:44 NKJV).

Let's push the pause button again. Think about this. How long has this man been in the leper colony, dwelling amongst the walking dead, mourning his own funeral? Who knows when the last time was that he'd been able to embrace his love. Or when he last sat down to dinner with his family. Not to mention the last time he was able to worship his God with his fellow man in the

It really brings an interesting picture to mind, doesn't it?

synagogue. *Now he can.* Because of Jesus' touch. And the first thing Jesus says to him is, "Don't say anything"?

There is no rehab with Jesus! His touch is complete.

Seriously?

We'd think the Master Artist would want to remove this canvas from the local art museum and display it in the town square.

We'd be off and running, wouldn't we? We'd go see our family and friends. We'd run to praise God in church. We'd hug everybody we came in contact with, just because we could! It's been too long.

But, Jesus says, **"Don't!"**

Is this some cruel trick? Complete restoration. A genuine miracle. But don't tell anyone. What's this all about?

> "...but go your way, show yourself to the priest..."
> (Mark 1:44 NKJV).

Jesus commands him to go to the priest. The priests would be in the temple. Not simply the synagogue.

Remember where we see this event taking place? In the region surrounding Capernaum.

Where's the temple? Jerusalem.

It's nearly 90 miles from Capernaum to Jerusalem! Jesus is telling him to make a 90-mile trip to the priest.

Remember, this is a man who had been *full* of leprosy. He was in the advanced stages; he had dwelt outside the camp. He'd been malnourished, thrown away and perhaps forgotten.

And now, the first thing Jesus tells him to do: Go 90 miles on foot to Jerusalem to present yourself to the priest!

Why does that matter?

There is no rehab with Jesus!

His touch is complete.

He not only made this man whole, but also fit.

If He tells the previous leper to make this physically demanding journey to Jerusalem to fulfill a purpose, then we have to believe He made him able to do it! No physical rehabilitation. Muscles that had atrophied are now well enough to travel 90 miles. *Simply by making the trip, he will prove the healing is real.*

"...*and offer for your cleansing those things which Moses commanded...*"
(Mark 1:44 NKJV).

The journey has a purpose: to be pronounced clean by the religious leadership of this day. Just as leprosy is described in the law there are also certain things that need to be accomplished in order to be considered cleansed or healed. For further insight you can check out Leviticus 14.

And the Significance?

"...*as a testimony to them...*"
(Mark 1:44 NKJV).

A testimony is a statement or declaration of a witness. A witness offers testimony as evidence in support of a fact or statement. In other words, a testimony is given by a witness to provide proof.

A testimony is a statement or declaration of a witness.

This is a phrase Mark uses two other times in his gospel. Whenever he uses this phrase it's always used in the context of opposition. You could say it's used in a hostile sense and always in a confrontational manner. The next time we see it is in Mark 6:11 in the midst of Jesus' instructions, as He's sending out the 12 disciples to proclaim the Kingdom. The last time we see it, is during His message about the end times in Mark 13:9.

A Confrontational Declaration

Realize that at this point in time the religious leadership—the priests—had rejected John the Baptist. Now they're rejecting Jesus and His message. Things just weren't measuring up to them. They wanted it their way.

So now we see that Jesus was sending them a witness according to the law. In other words, He was sending them testimony—proof that would fit their expectations. He was sending one to testify *according to what Moses commanded.* This would be the acceptable proof of who He was.

Think about this: If the priests were to recognize the leper as being cleansed, they'd also have to admit the vehicle of his cleansing. But, if they were to reject the healed man, then ultimately they'd reject the vehicle of his cleansing as well. They'd have to decide who Jesus was. If they admitted Jesus cleansed the leper, then He was the One they had been waiting for. If not, they would reject Him.

It's a powerful confrontation.

It's also a decision each one of us has to make. Let's flash forward to Mark 8:27-33 for just a moment. Jesus asks His disciples two very powerful questions: "Who do men say that I am?" The answers were all over the map—everything from Elijah (who never died), to John the Baptist come back to life, a good prophet, a great teacher, a nice man, a healer.

Then Jesus asked the disciples the question that all of mankind will someday have to answer: "And who do YOU say that I am?"

Is Jesus actually who He claims to be? The Messiah, the One who forgives sins and restores broken lives? Is He the Son of the Most High God, Jehovah? If so, and if you choose to believe that, it will affect your entire life. Because if He IS, and as we've seen—He has authority over evil and sickness and has the ability and desire to make us whole—He can certainly handle your day-to-day obstacles.

Cast the net.

Draw the net.

Leave behind the mundane. The brokenness.

Choose to follow and attach yourself to Him.

You don't have to descend to the lowest.

The One from the highest—your Master—willingly descends to where you are and picks you up, embraces you and restores your brokenness; if you'll let Him.

The Confrontation That Never Happened

The cleansed leper would be the direct confrontation of the priests in this hour. How would they respond? This is critical! It will be an essential, crucial moment with those who oppose Jesus. They will *have* to declare who He is. They will decide in what and whom they believe.

Just a few minutes ago, the leper was the outcast. Now, he's restored.

Before, he was one with no potential. Now, Jesus has commissioned him.

He was the reject. Now, he's the selected witness!

From outcast to testimony.

What a purpose.

What potential.

What a position.
What a testimony.
What a witness.

Here it Comes

Is there any higher office? He was the selected witness!

"However,..."
(Mark 1:45 NKJV).

Wait a minute.
Are you kidding?
You can't be serious.
One of *those* words?

> *"However, he went out and began to proclaim it freely,*
> *and to spread the matter..."*
> *(Mark 1:45 NKJV).*

This changes everything. Introduced by a conjunction, the atmosphere has totally changed. We've gone from the ecstasy of expectation to the destruction of defiance. When it seems he couldn't reach any higher plain, he chooses the low road.

The leper disobeys the Healer.

The broken subject ignores the Artist. He blurs his own paint.

It's easy to feel sorry for him. Surely he was overcome with excitement having received a renewed license on life. Maybe he just didn't get it. Or, maybe he just didn't care.

The broken subject ignores the Artist. He blurs his own paint.

Doesn't it *look* right? When Jesus touches our lives we should want to tell the world what He has done for us. It's natural. It seems like the proper thing to do. But remember, Jesus said, "Don't." And, He meant it. It doesn't matter how it may appear to others, or that it seemed like the natural thing to do. It's simply disobedience. And disobedience always costs.

From Susie:

I love extreme vacations—the farther and more remote, the better. I love finding places to visit that many have never heard of. So a few years ago, I asked an adventurous friend of mine to join me on an extreme adventure to Irian Jaya. If you look on a map, it's the farthest you can go without starting to circle back and head home. If you read about Irian Jaya in the travel books, it's described as "the most remote place on the planet." Some parts still boast cannibalism.

On our way to Irian Jaya, we decided to spend a few days in Bali. It's an amazing island nestled on the Indian Ocean. We were excited to purchase Batik dresses for $3 and to explore the island outside of our Holiday Inn (I'm all for remote vacations, but I still want my clean sheets and air-conditioning…and spaghetti!).

I love the water. And adventure. Mix the two together and I'm one happy camper. When we saw the jet-skis, we didn't have to look twice. Fifty dollars for a good 30 minutes in the pristine waters of the Indian Ocean was an amazing deal.

Let's Go!

I'm naturally an impatient person. I know I need to work on that, but to be honest, I'm afraid to pray for patience, because I'm concerned God might give it to me. I don't want it. I don't have time for it. (I know. More I need to pray about!)

I threw on my life jacket and ran to my jet ski only to be stopped by its Indonesian owner belting out instructions. *Does he think I'm a dumb American? I've ridden lots of jet-skis before.* Okay, I'd jet-skied twice. But I was anxious to get in the water and was sure I didn't need to know whatever he was jabbering about.

What's he saying? Something about staying away from the reef. His words drifted onto the water as I slid onto the damp seat of my ski with Kathy on her ski beside me. Kathy realized I hadn't paid much attention to the instructions, so she screamed, "He told us to stay away from the reef, Sooz." She full-throttled to the left, as I headed out to a giant dark spot in the distance that looked interesting, adventurous and mysterious. I was there within two minutes.

Stuck.

Gunning the motor, but not moving.

Oh. So this must be the reef.

I had run straight into it.

Kathy circled at a distance screaming, "You've hit the reef!"

"Yeah, I figured that out."

"He said to stay *away* from the reef or you'd get stuck!"

"Yeah, I know that! Help me get outta here."

"No, I'll get stuck, too."

So while she spent the next 25 minutes jet-skiing, I sat frustrated in what should have been a once-in-a-lifetime experience. Waiting. Fuming. Gunning the engine again. Flooding the jet ski.

Stuck.

In the reef.

Disobedience always costs. It cost me $50 for a two-minute ride.

It cost me the fun of scooting across the Indian Ocean.

It cost me the embarrassment of the Indonesian owners having to come get me and tow me back to shore. *I've proved them right,* I thought. *I've acted like a dumb American who didn't know any better.*

Disobedience always costs.

Because of the leper's disobedience, the priests were never confronted on this day.

The proof was never offered.

Testimony was never given.

The witness never took the stand.

And...

"Jesus could no longer openly enter the city, but was outside in deserted places"
(Mark 1:45 NKJV).

Obstructed

The kingdom work is hindered. Jesus has to retreat from the hysteria this man has created. He is slowed from fulfilling the purpose He set out to fulfill in verse 38. He has exchanged places with the leper.

Disobedience effects everything, everyone. There are personal consequences. But there are corporate ramifications as well.

Because of one man's act of disobedience, the work is hindered.

Unbelievable.

Pathetic.

Sad.

Choose any negative adjective—they all work here

Disobedience always costs.

Going Deeper
(To be answered individually or with a small group.)

- Have you answered the essential question of who Jesus is? Who is He to your circle of friends? Your fellow employees? Who is He to you?
- Describe how believing that Jesus really IS all He claims to be, will affect your entire life.
- Identify a time when disobedience cost you.
- Put yourself in the leper's place. Would you have obeyed Jesus and made the journey to the priests to show your healing? Or would you have enjoyed your healing and gone about your way?
- This is a metaphor for the Cross. The leper's condition is comparable to our sin condition. He was outside the community; We are outside the Kingdom. Jesus exchanged places with us. He left the Kingdom, went to the Cross and made the payment for our sins, so we could enter the Kingdom whole and restored. Have you accepted His payment for your sins? Share your salvation experience.
- Our response to Him is necessary for Him to complete His masterpiece. How am I responding to Him? How do my responses affect those around me?
- In a hostile world, we are proof or testimony of who Jesus is. What proof am I offering of who Jesus is?

Prayer time: Father, I never want to hinder Your work. Tenderize my heart. Help me to know Your voice better and better. When You speak, I want to recognize Your voice immediately and respond in obedience. Amen

CHAPTER
EIGHT

In various parts of the world, it takes effort to get to a church.

It takes risking your life to worship Christ.

How hard is it for you to reach Him?

If you're living in North or South America, it's easy to proclaim your faith, go to church, and draw closer to Him.

So why aren't we doing it?

GET TO JESUS

(Luke 5:17-39; Mark 2:1-4)

From Billy:

John Stallings penned the words:

> *"Touching Jesus is all that really matters,*
> *then your life will never be the same.*
> *There is only one way to touch Him,*
> *just believe when you call on His name."*

I hadn't thought about that song for years, until one night at a revival meeting in northeast Ohio when it flooded my memory.

It had been a good week. The crowds were good, services lively, and the Spirit of God was present. People had been responding, and lives had been changed. Masterpieces' restored.

It was the last night of the meeting and a spontaneous testimony service erupted. It was beautiful. People stood to share what God had been doing in their lives. You could sense a genuine atmosphere of praise.

Her Testimony

And then she stood. Her face was worn and tired. She stood with her shoulders slightly bent. Her dress was very common. I'll confess, I don't remember her name, however, I'll never forget what she said.

Her voice trembled as she spoke. She shared how difficult

the past few years had been—especially the last year. I listened intently as she described how her husband of 60-plus years lost his battle to Alzheimer's Disease. Her family had deserted her and now she was facing sickness herself. Yet, she had a testimony.

She relayed to all in the sanctuary that night that God had been her constant and proven to be true through it all. She continued her story and with a stronger, more determined voice concluded with this statement that has stuck with me:

"The last few years have been so very hard. However, I know this is true: The promises that are before me are greater than the pain of my past! You see, I have Jesus, and He's all I need."

That's when I realized this woman had touched Jesus. The memory of this song from my childhood replayed in my mind.

"Touching Jesus is all that really matters."

My Turn

Can I confess to you—there are so many times I think of everything else, but this. I come to a church service thinking about what I'm going to preach, how the music will go, wondering who's going to show up. Consumed by so many things—everything except the most important: touching Jesus.

I hope that statement's not too shocking. I feel I can confess this, because you're likely the same way. I mean, we all live lives in a very real world. There are occupational issues, family concerns and obligations that want to occupy our time and thoughts. If we're not careful, these things will control us.

I need this reminder; perhaps you do, too. Touching Jesus is all that really matters. If we'll touch Him, our lives will never be the same.

"And again He entered Capernaum after some days"
(Mark 2:1NKJV).

Jesus had retreated from the hysteria that had been created by the disobedience of one man. A man, who had known His touch and who had been miraculously restored, did exactly what he was told *not* to do. Because of this, Kingdom work was hindered.

What comes to mind when you read the words, "after some days" in Scripture? Perhaps you think of a short time span. For instance, as a fulltime evangelist, I'm (Billy) normally with a congregation for *some days:* I arrive on Sunday and leave Wednesday night after our closing service.

As a fulltime evangelist and speaker, I'm (Susie) usually with a congregation *some days*—but it's a bit shorter. I usually fly in to speak on Friday evening and leave Sunday afternoon. I'm with a women's conference or a church *some days*.

Or, maybe you think of the weekend: You work or attend class from Monday to Friday, counting the hours until you have some days off. A short span of time. **That's not what's being said here.**

In his book, *The Life and Times of Jesus the Messiah,* Albert Edersheim states:

"The second journey of Jesus through Galilee had commenced in

autumn; the return to Capernaum was 'after days,' which, in common Jewish phraseology, meant a considerable interval. As we reckon, it was winter.[2]"

In other words, this isn't just a few days. It's a significant period of time. Jesus goes to the wilderness in autumn, and now that winter is in full force, He returns to the city. This was a 'considerable' amount of time. This is very important for us to understand.

"...and it was heard that He was in the house"
(Mark 2:1 NKJV).

Rumor Has It

After a considerable amount of time, it was "heard" He had come back to the city. Simply heard. Translations vary in how this is stated: noised, reported, the news spread quickly, rumored, stated.

So, what we're about to see is simply the result of noise. Understand, this is not an eyewitness account. It wasn't someone walking down the road one evening and happened to see Jesus sitting on the porch drinking a Coke. Neither was it someone who saw a silhouette walk through the door of the home and recognized His swagger. This is not based upon confirmed sightings. It's simply rumor.

Amazing. Why?

Watch the response of this noise:

"Immediately many gathered together, so that there was no longer room to receive them, not even near the door"
(Mark 2:2 NKJV).

As soon as it's rumored, they flood the place! They come out to

---

2   Edersheim, A. (1896). *The Life and Times of Jesus the Messiah* (Vol. 1, p. 501). Bellingham, WA: Logos Bible Software.

Because of his disobedience, Kingdom work has been hindered.

see for themselves. In fact, so many people come that they're packed together in the living room like sardines. They're standing shoulder-to-shoulder, all eager to hear what Jesus has to say. They're spilling out the front door and huddling around the windows. They want the opportunity to look into His face. If something incredible happened, they wanted a front row seat. Their curiosity is evident. They hear the rumor. They come.

What does Jesus do?

> "...and He preached the word to them"
> (Mark 2:2 NKJV).

He reveals the canvas.

The Kingdom's going public.

This is why He came.

Remember, He revealed His purpose to the disciples back in Mark 1:38. But the work had been hindered by the healed leper who was told to quietly show himself to the priest instead of talking about what had happened. He did exactly the opposite: Instead of going to the priest, he bragged in public. And because of his disobedience, Kingdom work has been hindered.

But it's winter now.

A new season has arrived.

And Jesus seizes the opportunity to advance the Kingdom.

There's no concert, no magic show.

No product table with T-shirts or leather-banded crosses.

No strobes, no smoke, no opening act.

Just the Basics

Jesus simply preaches the Word to them.
It would have been an exciting place to be.
To see Him. To hear His voice. To bask in His presence. We
watch as the crowd is captivated by His message. They're
hanging on every syllable coming from His mouth.
They're drawn in by His passion.

But behind the scenes there's another story that's beginning to
unfold. It's a story that's happening across town.

Another Broken Person

"Then they came to Him, bringing a paralytic who was carried by four men"
(Mark 2:3 NKJV).

This story is one that has been filled with heartache and
struggle. We're not sure when it began, but obviously, it's been going on
for quite some time. Another smeared life turned upside on the Artist's
canvas. What has happened?

He's a paralytic. In other words, his body doesn't work. No
movement in his arms. No strength in his legs. His limbs are dead;
useless.

He's broken.

We don't know how he ended up like this. It could be that he
was born this way. Maybe he was dropped on his head as a child. Or
perhaps it was the result of a tragic accident later in life. How he arrived
here is unknown. He's just here: paralyzed, dependent, pathetic.

Jesus—the One who speaks authority over evil, chases sickness
away, touches the untouchables—is across town.

Was there a stirring in the paralytic's heart to get to the Artist? Were thoughts rushing through his mind of getting to where Christ was? Or did his friends simply insist that he go? Perhaps he was embarrassed. After all, he can't feed or bathe himself, or go for a walk. He could never get to where Jesus was. Not on his own. What a pitiful state. Just lying there. It was his sentence. It was his life.

Touching Jesus was all that mattered.

However, the story doesn't end there.

We meet four men. They're nameless men.

No titles or position. But they have huge hearts.

They define the word *friendship.*

When the paralytic couldn't get to where Jesus was, they took him. What this poor man could not do for himself, they would do for him.

Matt carriers. That's who they are.

Burden bearers.

The Greek word *pheró* (fer'-o) can be translated: to bring, bear, carry, or carry a burden. That's what his life had become—a burden. He was a burden not only to himself, but to others as well.

A burden. And the burden has become much too heavy. So they go to the only place they know. They bear the burden across town.

Jesus Was in the House.

Touching Jesus was all that mattered.

So they bring him to Jesus.

You see, if Jesus would touch a leper, certainly He can meet this need.

If He could banish sickness, disease and evil, then paralysis is no challenge.

They're so desperate for a genuine encounter with Jesus, they're willing to do *anything* to make it happen! Let's highlight this. It's an important fact.

They are so desperate to get to Jesus they're willing to do WHATEVER IT TAKES.

Do you know God absolutely loves it when we're desperate for Him? Oh, how that blesses Him! Flash forward to Luke 18:35-43. We see this same kind of desperation in the blind man beside the road. He's so desperate

He's desperate for wholeness.

for a genuine encounter with Jesus, he starts shouting, "Son of David, have mercy on me!"

He's an outcast. Just like this paralytic.

People consider him a freak. Just like this paralytic.

He's desperate for wholeness. Just like this paralytic.

Jesus is so moved by the blind man's desperation that in spite of all the other things vying for His attention, He stops in front of the blind man and heals him.

Have you experienced this kind of desperation? Are you so spiritually desperate for a genuine encounter with Jesus that you're willing to do WHATEVER IT TAKES to experience Him?

If so, then you can identify with the four guys who were desperate to get to Jesus.

Whatever it Would Take

> *"And when they could not come near Him because of the crowd..."*
> *(Mark 2:4 NKJV).*

They start their journey. Gently—but firmly—they each take a corner of the mat that's connected to wooden poles and lift. They begin to carry this man to the place where Jesus is. How far did they have to walk? Was it a few blocks or a few miles?

Obviously, the distance wasn't a concern to them. The issue? *Get to Jesus!* Their arms became fatigued. Pain seared through their lower backs, and they realized how difficult it is to carry a human across rocky paths,

up hills,

down dusty roads,

and through narrow streets.

Finally they reach the home.

Now, their hearts sink.

They see the house and the crowd spilling out the door and huddling around the windows. How will they ever get inside? They realize the nature of the crowd and the status of a paralytic. They have to try.

Jesus was in the house!

Touching Him is all that matters. They edge their way to the door. Desperation has now become personified.

It's their heartbeat. It's the sweat on their brows.

It's the agony piercing through their strained muscles.

They inch their way along the outside, but the crowd is ruthless.

Someone screams, "Hey! We were here first."

Another, "If we could move forward, we would! We can barely see and hear what's going on. Stop pushing."

They can't get in.

Pain seared through their lower backs, and they realized how difficult it is to carry a human.

They don't give up.

Desperation's heartbeat only pulsates faster.

Rocks inside their open-foot sandals have rubbed their feet raw.

Their palms, sweaty and burdened from the weight, slip on the poles holding the mat. The four men tighten their grip and clench their teeth in conjunction with the muscle spasms. They are burden bearers.

Jesus is in the house!

They will not give up.

Desperation is alive.

> "...they uncovered the roof where He was..."
> (Mark 2:4 NKJV).

Unstoppable

They exert the effort to carefully carry this man up the stairs toward the flat roof. Desperation pushes each one of the eight individual feet up each stair.

The mat hits the wall.

One of the four men trips.

Regaining their balance, they continue up the stairs until finally reaching the roof. They're actually on top of the house!

Let's watch as they lay this man down. No time is wasted. They immediately spring into action. They're surveying the roof, trying to find the exact location where Jesus is teaching. It wouldn't do any good to lower him toward the back or middle of the house. They've already seen the crowd's response. That won't be good enough. They need to get to Jesus.

When they find where He is, their action continues as they begin prying loose the tiles with their bare hands.

It's hard work.

It's painful work.

Fingernails are turned back.

Flesh is sliced as they uncover the roof.

But the price is worth the cost as they work to get this man to Jesus.

"So when they had broken through..."
(Mark 2:4 NKJV).

When the tiles are removed, the thatch that makes up the roof is exposed. They will *not* allow this barrier to stop them.

Jesus is in the house.

Touching Him is all that matters.

Desperation.

On all fours—and with Navy Seal Team Six precision—they begin to remove the barrier. With bare hands they dig. And they dig. And they dig.

Can you imagine being on the inside of the house at this point? You're captivated by Jesus' presence. You're hanging on His every word. Then, you begin to hear scratching from the roof. Squirrels? Raccoons?

You try to ignore it when something suddenly hits your shoulder. You brush it away as another piece hits you on the head. What in the... All of a sudden another piece hits the ground as light begins to shine down. Your attention is now focused upward as you watch dust particles in the light coming from a hole in the roof!

The roof is caving in. The crowd pushes back as you see four sets of hands tearing through the roof; four sets of hands digging through until they begin to lower a mat right to the feet of Jesus.

Target Reached

> *"...they let down the bed on which the paralytic was lying"*
> *(Mark 2:4 NKJV).*

Hanging over the edge of the hole, they begin to carefully lower this man to Jesus' feet.

Jesus was in the house.

Touching Him was all that mattered.

When the crowd wouldn't let them through the door, they uncovered the roof.

They had to get to the Artist.

What an incredible picture.

What beautiful desperation.

Let's Get Personal

We have a lot to consider with this, don't we? First of all, these four men give us a magnificent picture of genuine friendship. They also demonstrate their willingness to be burden bearers. And they display an intense desperation to have a legitimate encounter with Jesus.

Jesus was in the house.

We also learn a lot from the paralyzed man's situation. When it seemed impossible for him to get to Jesus, Jesus moved the right men into his life to bring him to the Great Physician.

Can you relate?

It's about you.

At times, does it feel as though the distance between you and Jesus is just too far?

The journey too difficult?
The odds stacked against you are too high?
That's why sometimes we need a little help from friends.
Real friends will move you closer to Jesus.
Whatever it takes.

Going Deeper

(To be answered individually or with a small group.)

• Have you been a burden bearer for someone? Describe the situation.
• Describe what a genuine encounter with Jesus Christ entails. Have you actually had a legitimate encounter with Him?
• How do you display spiritual desperation? Can Christians still have a spiritual desperation? Or is this a need that's met once and for all?
• What handicap in your life keeps you from intimacy with Christ? Are you willing to let the Great Physician handle it?
• How desperate are you to get to Jesus and allow Him to touch your deepest needs?
• It's OK to ask for help from Christian friends. What makes this hard for us? Will you put aside the, *I don't need anyone,* thought and ask for spiritual help when you need it?

Prayer time: Ask God to bring to your mind anything in your life that's keeping you from experiencing intimacy with Him. When you know what that is, place it under His control. Also, ask God to show you anyone who needs your help in being a "burden bearer."

CHAPTER
NINE

Embarrassed.

At the end of his rope.

A freak.

Never good enough.

Always wondering what others were thinking.

Can you relate?

If so, you'll identify to his astonishment when hearing the words of Christ.

To one who is devastated, inadequate and lost, the first word is all that matters.

THE FIRST WORD

(Mark 2:5)

From Billy:

I finally felt like myself again. Having only cancelled my spring and summer schedule, I stepped back into a full speaking tour the fall of 2006. I'll admit it was exciting. It felt good to be doing what I'd been called to do. I finally felt as though there was some normalcy in my life. I felt like myself again. After a hard, dark six months, dawn was breaking on the horizon. A new day was beginning.

I've always been an analytical person. I get a thought in my head and at times it consumes me. I guess you could say I have a one-track mind. I lay my head on my pillow at night and those thoughts begin to race and roll—especially now it seemed.

Even though I was traveling again, I couldn't escape the thoughts and feelings of failure. I'd go to my speaking engagements, present what I prepared and put on a happy face. Then, I'd go back to the hotel and it would begin: the voice of the enemy. The taunting of the discourager. The never-ending drumbeat of despair. It was always there, and it was hard to ignore.

I knew I had stepped back into what I'd been called by God to do. He had protected and preserved me through the dark night of separation and divorce. I realized God was taking what was meant for harm and using it to bring about something good. He was using the events of living to form me into the person I was becoming…who He wanted me to be.

But another battle was beginning. It was a battle that would continue for more than four years. A war was being waged in my mind and spirit. It was a battle like no other, and I almost allowed it to get the best of me.

He was tortured—not only by his condition, but also by his mindset. He was a paralytic. His body was useless. He couldn't do any of the things normal people would do. Simple things such as going for a walk, feeding himself, going to the restroom alone, cleaning himself and going to synagogue were all out of the question.

He was completely dependent upon others to complete these simple tasks we so easily take for granted. Physical needs can be tended to. Perhaps begrudgingly, but there would be those who would care enough to do what was necessary. They would bear the burden of another. They would tend to this man's physical needs.

We're more than just physical beings, however. We're packed with feelings, and powerful emotions. He was not exempt.

Of course no one can know—no one besides the man—what he was feeling. However, we *do* know how others felt about him. With the exception of his four genuine friends, others believed he was getting what he deserved. Surely his affliction was a penalty for a huge sin in his life. (Remember the question in John 9:1-5 that the disciples asked about the blind man: Is this man blind because of sin in his life or sin in his parents' lives?) It's the same idea as the leper; Because of sin in his life has God removed His hand of mercy?

This was payment.

This was deserved.

Memory Is a Powerful Thing

If you're told something long enough—regardless of reality—you begin to believe it. If a father tells his son he's stupid over and over again, he'll eventually believe it.

Memory is why elephants can be controlled with one small chain attaching one foot to a tree stump. When the elephant is still a baby, the owner chains it to something heavy, so he won't escape camp. It's free to roam during the day, but each night it's chained.

Eventually, the elephant grows in size, weight and strength. When the chain is put back on his foot and fastened to a small stump, he could easily pull the stump out of the ground or even break the chain. But because of the elephant's strong memory, he believes the chain is stronger than he is.

While his foot is chained, he forever is a prisoner to the chain.

While his foot is chained, he forever is a prisoner to the chain.

Transition to the paralytic.

For years he'd been chained to feelings of inadequacy.

He was tortured.

Ostracized. The name-calling. And so many questions.

Why him? Why this? Will it ever end?

Maybe the stain went much deeper. Maybe he knew what he'd done. If the paralysis was the result of some terrible accident later in life, perhaps he could point to the sin, the reason for this result. No one else might know, but he did. He felt he deserved it, that this was fair penalty.

If only he could go back…

make different decisions…

his life would be different.

The mat was a sentence—
a life sentence he would have to accept.

Taken to Jesus

He was tortured.

But Jesus was in the house.

They carry him to Jesus.

You remember the scene in our last chapter. We witnessed the effort of the four friends. Their care and concern was evident. But the house was overflowing. They *must* get to Jesus. This burden had become too much to bear. Touching Jesus was all that mattered.

The curiosity of the crowd kept them from getting through the door. The desperation of their circumstance and the determination not to let this opportunity pass, found them on the roof. They lay him down in the corner and spring into action. Removing the tile. Digging through the thatch and mortar. As they labor, he's once again alone with his thoughts.

Was he embarrassed? *I wish they wouldn't. I didn't ask for this.*

Was he angry? *You have no idea how I feel! And you're only making it worse!*

Was he self-conscious? *Once again, the center of attention. The stares never end.*

Was he grateful? *Thank you! You're enabling me to accomplish what I could never do on my own.*

He Was Confused

He probably felt a mixture of all the above. *Plus*—he felt judged.

Let's not lose sight of what's going on here. He was the punished—the outcast seemingly as judgment of God.

Now, he's had a stark reminder of how the people felt about him as they refused to let them pass through the door. He was able to hear the insults, to see the looks of disdain. It was simply the reality of his condition—the repeated percussion of worthlessness and despair.

Normal people don't act this way.

On top of this, the men who had carried him were now doing the unthinkable. They were tearing a hole in the roof. Do you realize how improper this action is?

Normal people don't act this way.

The roof is there for a reason.

It affords shelter from the elements and shade in the day.

It's protection from intruders of all kind and provides warmth on a cool night.

You simply don't destroy another's property.

What would the homeowners say?

What would they do?

This is completely out of line!

It's an Interruption

Don't forget what's going on inside the house—what they're about to interrupt. The Teacher is there. After all, that's why the crowd has come. This is a teacher unlike any other. He teaches as though He actually knows what He's talking about.

He speaks with authority.

Rabbis or teachers didn't like to be interrupted.

It wasn't looked upon favorably by either student or teacher.

But that's exactly what was going to happen.

Questions mounting.

An unclean, unwanted, unwelcome vandal. That's what he has become.

What would be the reaction of the crowd?

How would the homeowner respond?

What would the teacher do?

Tortured.

There's no other word for it.

He felt tortured.

It pulsated through his veins.

It taunted his thoughts.

It seared like a branding iron on soft skin.

All the questions would soon be answered. The men approach. With bleeding, dirty hands they take the corners of his prison. They lift and carry him to the hole they've made in the roof.

They lower him. In front of everybody, right to the feet of Jesus.

Look at him. Do you see the concern on his face? It's written all over. The fear? The worry? Life has treated him harshly.

Jesus saw.

Wow. Aren't you thankful we have a Jesus who's concerned about the entire individual? There it is: the benefit! Can you place yourself on that mat? It's all about you. You're center stage. Christ's eyes are focused on you.

He saw his physical need. There's no question about this. Everybody could see it. He's on a mat. His body is a twisted, tangled,

It's all about you. You're center stage. Christ's eyes are focused on you.

useless mess. After all, that's why they brought him here. He can't walk. He can't do anything. Physically, he's broken. His life had become nothing but a burden to himself and everyone else.

What Jesus Sees

Jesus sees beyond the exterior to the interior. He is aware of much more than just the physical brokenness of this man. Looking beyond the shell, He sees the isolation, hurt, questions and messy emotions. In other words, He sees the torture. He cares for the whole person.

Questions. Fears.

Feelings of inadequacy.

Torture.

How would the teacher respond?

All questions are answered as Jesus begins to speak.

> *When Jesus saw their faith, He said to the paralytic,*
> *"Son, your sins are forgiven you"*
> *(Mark 2:5).*

Did you hear it?

> *"Son..."*

That's how He begins. The first word He says is **son.**

That's a big deal.

You see, it really *is* about YOU.

May we pause here for just a minute?

If we're not careful we'll read right over and miss the beauty of what's going on. It's easy to assume this type of speech was common in Jesus' vernacular. But it wasn't.

This type of language is *familial* language. In other words, it's the language of family. In the context of Jewish society, in this biblical time, if you were referring to one as son, he was actually your son.

First and foremost He sees a heart that needs to be reconciled to his Father.

Or, if you called someone child or daughter, she really was your child or daughter. It's family talk. It's very intimate. And Jesus simply didn't talk like this often. He would use the word son if He were speaking of one's son, or daughter, if He were referring to one's daughter. But for Him to actually address someone as son or daughter was rare.

Three times.

That's all.

That's a big deal.

It's a really big deal when you begin to realize that the only times you hear Him talk like this is to the outcast, the unwanted, the insecure. The words come from His mouth as an embrace to a fearful child. In the midst of turmoil He speaks comfort, peace, reassurance. Such a beautiful sound!

The only other times Jesus does this is in Mark 5:34 and in John 13:33. We'll look at these two examples closer at the end of this chapter in the Going Deeper section.

They brought him to Jesus.

The callousness of the crowd made the house impenetrable.

A hole has been torn in the roof.

The instruction time of the Teacher has been interrupted.

The look of concern was on the man's twisted face.

Tortured.

Jesus sees this man. *Really sees him.* Sure, He sees his physical need. However, He's sees much more than that. First and foremost He sees a heart that needs to be reconciled to his Father. He'll deal with that for sure. His perception is perfect. There's nothing hidden. He sees the feelings of inadequacy, hears the questions from his heart of why?

The incorrect thinking was obvious and needed to be corrected. So with a word, He verbally caresses the discomfort, erases all concern and embraces him with His word.

Son.

The first word He says.

He knew him.

He loved him.

He called him son.

Jesus lifts the man from the mat emotionally before He ever lifts Him physically.

His word spoke life.

Just what He needed. Tortured no more.

From Billy:

I was losing the battle. I was overrun by the accusations from the enemy: *Who do you think you are? What gives you the right to stand and preach to anybody? Why should anyone listen to you? You're a failure! You couldn't even keep your marriage together. You're pathetic. You might as well quit.*

And I almost did. I'm thankful though, that when I felt like quitting, Jesus was unwilling to quit me.

It was June of 2010. I was participating in a training camp for summer interns involved with a ministry I am part of. The week is packed to the brim: three teaching times each morning and two worship and preaching sessions each night. I was so low I wasn't even able to speak. I'm ashamed to admit that, but it's where I was.

I don't know how you deal with things, but remember I

said earlier in my story that I'm a fixer. That's my personality. I can handle it. I can fix it. So, when I'm dealing with things, I want to be left alone. I become a recluse and I shut everybody out.

The Right Voice

I was staying with a number of guys who participated in this same ministry that week. We were sharing a home. I went to my room, closed the door and got into bed. All of a sudden, my door opened. Without a knock or announcement, my friend came into the room and sat down on the corner of my bed. He knew what I had gone through. He could tell I was in a battle. I believe Jesus led him into my room that night. This is what he said:

"Billy, you're listening to all the wrong voices. You're beginning to believe the lies of the enemy. **Why don't you allow Jesus to speak in your life the words He wants spoken?** Then, listen to His voice. Above every other voice, hear *Him*. And believe what He says. **Let Jesus speak into your life the words He wants spoken.**"

I'm so thankful for the boldness of a friend who was Jesus to me that night. I don't mind telling you that since that night this has become my prayer. In fact, I pray it numerous times each day.

Speak, Jesus, in my life the words You want spoken.
Help me hear Your voice above every other voice.
Help me believe what You speak.

I need to tell you that He is faithful. He has spoken. He continues to speak. I'm thankful that today I stand in victory! Not because of anything I've done, rather because of what He has spoken. I realize who I am. I know where I stand.

He knows me.

He loves me.

He calls me son.

Tortured no more. The battle is over. Victory has come.

He has spoken.

Jesus didn't place conditions. He didn't address the roof problem. He simply called him and bestowed complete restoration.

That's what the Master Artist does.

No need to feel inadequate any more.

Simply listen to His voice.

Son.

That's not halfway acceptance.

That's total.

Don't listen to the crowd, the enemy; don't even listen to your own doubts. Learn to focus on the Voice who calls you His own.

Going Deeper

(To be answered individually or with a small group.)

- The man on the mat felt tortured. He was an outcast. People looked on him in judgment—believing his disability was caused by his sin. Identify a time in your life when you felt tortured by things that weren't right in your life. How did you deal with it?

- Place yourself on the mat. What emotions would you be dealing with as four friends pick you up, and tear through the roof of a public building, interrupting a packed-out event?

- Let's take a look at the two other times Christ uses familial language. Read Mark 5:25-34. Why is this woman so desperate? Many Bible scholars believe she began bleeding at puberty. Let's assume that was age 13. It's been 12 years. She's 25 now. At this age, what *should* she be experiencing? Her money has been spent on quack remedies that haven't helped. But she hears Jesus is near and makes her way to Him, pushes her way through the crowd, and touches the hem of His garment.

  If you've given blood, you know the weakness you feel afterward. For one who has bled for twelve years, how easy or difficult do you think it was for her to get through the crowd and touch Jesus' robe? What emotions do you think she was feeling? When Jesus addressed her as "Daughter," what do you suppose went through her mind? Why do you think He called her that?

- Read John 13:21-33. What event is happening here? Why are the disciples so confused? What does Jesus call them? Why do you suppose He calls them that? Put yourself in the place of the disciples around the table with Jesus. If He addressed you this way, how would you feel?

- Describe a time you desperately needed a matt carrier—someone to bear your burden and do for you what you couldn't do for yourself. How did this make a difference for you?
- What voices are you listening to that are a positive influence on your life? (They encourage and affirm you. They speak words of truth.) What voices are you listening to that bring out the worst in yourself? What keeps you tuned in to them? Will you commit to focusing on His voice above all others?

Prayer time: Spend some time simply thanking God for the intimacy He provides. He calls you SON! DAUGHTER! Bask in His love. Ask Him to continue to draw you into deeper intimacy with Him.

CHAPTER
TEN

You're well aware you blew it.

No argument.

But now that you're guilty, how do you deal with it?

Does the guilt hit you in the stomach?

Does your head hurt?

Are you sleepless?

What do you do with the guilt?

Believe it: Your Father actually *wants* it.

Will you give it to Him?

FORGIVEN

(Mark 2:1-5)

From Susie:

My mother was scheduled for heart surgery at 7 a.m., so Dad and I left the house at 5 a.m., to make sure we were there in plenty of time to be with her before surgery. We wanted to pray with her and simply sit beside her as long as we could.

I was living in Colorado Springs, Colo., and flew home to Okla. City the day before. Dad and I agreed we'd drive separate vehicles to the hospital that morning so we could rotate being there throughout the day. He pulled out of the driveway and I backed out after him.

It was dark.

I was still sleepy.

I wasn't used to driving his truck.

As I backed out of the driveway, I heard it—the crunch of the side of his truck against the brick encasing the mailbox. My heart sank. How much damage had been done to the mailbox *and* the truck?

No time to stop, get out and assess the situation, we needed to get to the hospital. I continued to follow Dad. We parked in the visitor's lot, and I opened the door of the truck already beating myself up emotionally and feeling guilty beyond words.

We were so worried about Mom. The last thing Dad needed was a wrecked truck and mailbox to add to the list of concerns.

I locked the truck and felt the warmth of Dad's arm around my shoulders. "Honey, you couldn't see the mailbox, could you?"

Honey?

I felt as though it should've been, *Idiot! What in the world?*

But Dad wasn't like that. He never spoke harshly to anyone. And the time I needed reassurance the most—before my mom's delicate heart surgery—he took time to give it to me.

He understood.

He knew it was dark and that I wasn't used to driving a truck.

Honey. He wanted me to know it was okay.

"I'm so sorry, Dad. I thought I had more space. Look at this damage on the truck."

"It's only a truck, Honey. You're my daughter. And you're not hurt, so everything's fine."

When I returned to the house later, I noticed I'd completely taken out the brick enclosure for the mailbox. It cost a few hundred dollars to replace it. And it cost to get the truck fixed. But as we walked into the hospital, his arm around me, nothing else needed to be said. I was secure in my father's love.

What an incredibly captivating scene!

The house has been overrun by the crowd. Jesus' presence has captured their attention as He publicizes the Kingdom. The excitement level was out the roof—that was, until the roof was torn apart.

Attention was now focused upon a paralytic who had been lowered through a hole in the roof made by four men. The teaching time was over. At least that's how it appeared. In reality, the greatest lesson was about to be given. It was a lesson that would literally draw a line in the sand, shake the foundation of the religious establishment, and challenge the mindset of all who would hear.

It's the foundation that everything is built upon. This is the proposition of the Kingdom that's going public.

> *"He said to the paralytic, "Son, your sins are forgiven you"*
> *(Mark 2:5 NKJV).*

This is the statement He makes that will challenge the mindset of the religious world of that day. It's an incredible statement that we need to slow down and give careful attention.

First, remember to whom who He's talking:

> *"...He said to the **paralytic**..."*

The paralytic.
Getting exactly what he deserved.
The unclean. The unwanted. The judged. The unloved.
That's to whom who He was talking.
Next, notice how He says it:

> *"...your sins **are forgiven***

Pause

Let's spend a moment here to make sure we understand not only what's being said, but the manner in which it's being spoken. On the printed page we can't hear tone of voice, stressing of syllables or feeling behind the statement. We can't hear the spirit or mood in which the words are delivered.

It's easy to imagine that when the teaching time is interrupted, Jesus looks upon the pitiful sight of this man and in a boisterous voice commands that his sins be gone.

A command.

It's easy to hear that through the page.

But if that were the case, in the Greek language, it would be referred to as the imperative mood. The imperative mood is "the mood that normally expresses a command, intention, exhortation or polite request. The imperative mood is therefore not an expression of reality but possibility and volition."[3]

But…

The statement that Jesus makes isn't in this mood.

It's not a request.

Not a command.

Not a suggestion.

When Jesus says, "…sins are forgiven," it's in what's referred to as the *indicative mood.* What's the indicative? Simply what it sounds like: It's "the mood in which the action of the verb or the state of being it describes, is presented by the writer as real. It is the mood of assertion, where the writer portrays something as actual (as opposed to possible or contingent on intention)."[4]

In other words, when Jesus speaks these words, it's a statement of fact.

This is not up for debate.

This statement indicates fact.

This is reality.

---

3   Heiser, M. S., & Setterholm, V. M. (2013; 2013). *Glossary of Morpho-Syntactic Database Terminology.* Logos Bible Software.
4   Heiser, M. S., & Setterholm, V. M. (2013; 2013). *Glossary of Morpho-Syntactic Database Terminology.* Logos Bible Software.

Sins are forgiven.

That's how He says it.

Now, let's look at what He says.

Remember how He begins:

"*...Son...*"

Son.

That's how He begins.

It Had to Feel Good

In a world hardened to the reality of
his condition, the first word he heard was
son. The language of the family. An embrace.
It's a powerful scene that captured the
attention and the judgment of the crowd.

Jesus speaks, and he is lifted.

Most importantly, it would have gripped the heart of the man
imprisoned to the mat. Jesus speaks, and he is lifted. Not physically, but
emotionally.

Jesus cared.

Really cared.

About the whole person.

"*...your* **sins** *are forgiven you.*"

Sin.

That's a heavy subject.

To appreciate what Jesus is saying we need to spend a little time
here. Do you remember how we began our journey? All the way back at
the beginning? How things were intended to be? Let's do a quick recap.

Let's go back to the day when the Creator God formed man in His image, filled him with His spirit and

The Master Artist filling the center of His canvas with color, rhythm, vibrancy.

placed Him in a Garden He designed. Man was His masterpiece: A loving Father gazing into the soul of His creation willing to do *whatever it would take* to help him become all He dreamed for him. The Master Artist filling the center of His canvas with color, rhythm, vibrancy. A passionate Creator breathing, "It's all about you, My child. I'll give My very life for you."

And then He spoke a word of freedom: complete freedom. The only requirement? Don't eat from the tree that's in the center of the Garden: Stay away from the Tree of Knowledge of Good and Evil. Don't eat of it because if you do, you'll die. A God-centered existence. Every need would be supplied. Man only needed to love God enough to obey.

We understand that forced relationship is not relationship at all. There needed to be an expression of man's love for God. And that expression would be to not eat of the tree. Obedience.

Love = Obedience

Let's put it this way: The mark of true love is complete, unconditional obedience to God's leadership in your life. It always has been and always will be. That means our lives will reveal how much we love Him by the level of our obedience to His voice. In that obedience He continues to complete you: His masterpiece.

You know the story. Tempted by the enemy, man and woman chose to eat from the tree. He chose to do what God told him not to do. (This is really important: They knew not to do it and they did it anyway.)

In that act, when they disobeyed God's voice—His command—relationship was broken. They had sinned. They shifted from being God-centered to self-centered. The colors ran, the painting began to fade, the masterpiece seemed lost.

There is nothing more offensive to God than sin.

It breaks relationship.

It breaks His heart.

Up to this point in the story Jesus has been displaying His authority—over mankind, the realm of truth, the spiritual realm, over sickness and disease of all kinds. There is one area He has left untouched. It's an area that would be considered the cause of all the above effects. Sickness and disease were directly related to it. Demonic possession was a result. But now, He goes to the heart of the matter. That which had separated, broken what was intended, must now submit.

Jesus announces authority over sin itself when He makes the statement of fact:

"...sins are forgiven..."

What has been marred, can be restored.

What is broken, can be put back together.

What was intended can be realized.

The Kingdom Is Going Public

This is a Kingdom unlike what had been established by the religious world of the day. The God of this Kingdom is not a God who would pick and choose insiders and outsiders. He didn't find His delight in causing some to be diseased, broken, paralyzed. All are welcome.

The foundation of the Kingdom is found in the statement of fact that Jesus makes: SINS ARE FORGIVEN.

This means you are never too far…

never in so deep…

never so paralyzed that the Master cannot restore what was intended!

That's such wonderful news. He is focused on you.

That's reality.

It's such great news that Matthew expresses it like this: (Jesus says to the paralytic.)

"Son, be of good cheer; your sins are forgiven you."

Cheer up!

The Creator is at work.

Sins are forgiven.

Accept it.

Going Deeper

(To be answered individually or with a small group.)

- Describe what it felt like when you first discovered that Christ wanted to forgive your sins.
- What adjectives can you use to explain how you feel to know that it's a FACT: If you seek Christ's forgiveness and repent of your sins, He will forgive and cleanse?
- Christ called the paralyzed man "Son." What other names do you suppose he may have been called?
- What are favorite names of endearment you enjoy having family call you?
- Before Christ healed the man physically, He lifted him emotionally. Identify an area in your life where you need to be lifted emotionally.

Prayer time: Father, I can't tell you how good it feels to be in Your family and to be called by the family name of son or daughter. I don't want to take this privilege for granted. As I live in obedience to You, consistently remind me that I belong to You.

CHAPTER
ELEVEN

They're always around.

They're the people who criticize and talk in low tones and spread gossip.

They're intimidating, and we often find ourselves trying to gain their approval.

They seem to have an air of authority.

They're quick to accuse, and they ask questions laced with judgment.

How can one who hasn't been to art school create a canvas extraordinaire?

It all depends on who holds the brush.

FROM THEIR HEARTS
(Mark 2-3:6)

We've met several people on the Artist's canvas. We've been inside their stories. There's one group, however, that we haven't met. Do you remember reading about the day Jesus was teaching in the synagogue? Do you remember the response of the crowd that heard Him? They were astonished. Why? Because, "He taught as one having authority, and not as *the scribes*."

There they are.

The scribes.

The religious leadership.

Those who were entrusted with the Law.

The protectors.

The proclaimers.

Now, they make their entrance. From the minute we see them, they're constantly trying to upstage the main actor. They're battling for center stage. The struggle ensues. The drama builds.

The Source

It's important that we remember what's taken place up to this point. In chapter one, Jesus has burst upon the scene after John the Baptist was rejected and imprisoned. He's proclaiming His Father's Kingdom—He's displaying the canvas. In other words, the Kingdom's on display. It's going public.

We have learned of His identity through the authority He displays. We've learned that Jesus is the *Source of Authority*. He has authority over every realm. He's been displaying His authority over sickness

Jesus is the Source of Authority.

and disease of all kinds. He speaks to demons and they must obey His voice. He teaches as though He knows what He's talking about. He has authority over the realm of truth. He *is* the Source of Authority.

Now there's a shift that begins to occur. Where He had been revealing His identity through the authority He displays, now He begins to reveal this Kingdom He has come to proclaim. With every scene we learn a little bit more of what this Kingdom is all about and find that it stands in stark contrast to the kingdom that had been established by the religious leadership of the day. The two do not go together.

In other words: You don't simply add Jesus to your life.

He must *become* your life.

You don't add Him to your religious system.

He must *replace* that system.

The Master Artist isn't about collecting artwork; He only has one piece. It's in motion. It's fluid. You're on the canvas in vibrancy.

It's a new way of living. It's a new kingdom reality. Jesus begins to shake the foundation of the religious world.

They don't like it.

It changes everything.

The conflict begins.

From this point on we'll hear the dissonance between this group and Jesus. We'll watch as they continually challenge Him as the two kingdoms collide. It crescendos throughout the rest of this section, finally reaching its climax in Mark 3:6.

"Conflict narratives" — that's probably what these next five stories are best termed. Let's watch as it begins.

Back at the House

We rewind a moment to comprehend the details that advance

us forward. After being in the wilderness for an extended period of time, Jesus makes His way back to the city. Rumor has it that He's there, so the house is flooded with people. The Kingdom's going public, so Jesus preaches the Kingdom to the gathered crowd.

> *There's a big difference in being religious and being Christian.*

While this is going on, four men bring the paralytic to Jesus. When they can't get through the front door they tear a hole in the roof and lower him to Jesus' feet.

Jesus sees their faith and speaks.

He articulates the proposition of the Kingdom.

The foundation for everything else that follows.

Sins are forgiven.

Then, we meet them:

> *"And some of the scribes were sitting there..."*
> *(Mark 2:6NKJV).*

Let's pause for a minute. Isn't it amusing the first time we meet this group we see them "sitting there"? Sure, it's the proper posture for a time like this, but it's a humorous picture.

There's a big difference in being religious and being Christian. The two are not the same. If you're going to follow Jesus, you won't be able to do it sitting down. He's always on the move. He's always intentional. To be in the center of what He's up to simply means you'll be on the move, and you'll be intentional as well.

On the other hand, religious people are really good at sitting there. You can count on this: If you sit there long enough, you'll do what comes naturally: complain. Usually the complaining is about what others are or aren't doing. They won't lift a finger to do it themselves, but they'll complain.

It begins.

They hear the proposition Jesus makes.

Conflict begins.

When Jesus makes this statement you can only fall on one of two sides. Either He has the authority to make this proclamation or

Either He has the authority to make this proclamation or He's out of His mind.

He's out of His mind. He can either speak as the representative of the Kingdom or He's a blasphemer and belongs nailed to a tree. No in-between. We quickly learn where the religious leadership lands.

Ouch

Understand that these men's pride is already hurt. In a modern context we would say that these were the guys who had attended seminary. Maybe they had their own television broadcasts. They had graduate degrees. They had earned the right of their position.

Now Jesus bursts upon the scene and the people are saying that He's a better teacher. He actually sounds like He knows what He's talking about. A carpenter from Nazareth. Can anything good come from Nazareth? There's no doubt: Their pride is hurt.

The Artist has created a Masterpiece, yet He hasn't been to art school.

This is a powerful introduction. Throughout the rest of this section we'll discover these men a little more in each story. Jesus will do something, and they'll respond.

Their response in the first four stories (through the end of Mark chapter two) is to ask Jesus a question. Each question can be whittled down to a *why*.

Through the rest of this chapter let's follow the progression of these questions. Let's meet these men and understand who they are and what drives their actions. We're going to briefly look at each question.

They're sitting there.

Jesus makes the statement, "Son, your sins are forgiven you."

Their response:

"And some of the scribes were sitting there and reasoning in their hearts,
'Why does this Man speak blasphemies like this?
Who can forgive sins but God alone?'"
(Mark: 2:6-7 NKJV).

Question #1

Why does He talk like this? Only God can forgive sins.

By the way, they're telling the truth. In the sin business, God is the offended party. Only He can grant forgiveness. That's how it works.

When you're seeking forgiveness, only the one who's offended can grant what you're seeking. But remember, Jesus is laying the foundation for His Father's Kingdom. He's saying, "God forgives your sins."

Notice where the question begins: in their hearts. It starts on the inside.

Let's look at the second conflict narrative: We see and hear the calling of Levi (also called Matthew), the tax collector. After that call, the scene changes, and we're at a party. It's a party that's being thrown in Jesus' honor, by the one whose life had been changed. It's an exciting scene. Jesus is reclining at the table along with His disciples, Levi, and several tax collectors and sinners. Revival has come to town!

If we're not careful we might think there's a group that's not represented: the religious leadership. We'd think that because they're not there. Well, they're not in the house at the table. They'd never do that. These people of the dirt were below them. They'd never associate with the riff raff, never attend a sinner's party like this. But they are there. Look closely.

They're on the outside looking in.

They're gathering around the windows.

They see what's going on.

There's Jesus. And there are the people of the dirt.

They're eating. They're laughing. They're smacking each on the back. The Artist is collaborating with His creation.

Question #2

Why does He act like this?

This is really an accusation. It's more of a statement in Greek: "With tax collectors and sinners He eats!" That's what they're saying over and over. They're outraged. Notice the progression: They're on the outside looking in. It started on the inside, within their hearts and now it's working its way to the fringes.

The scribes are fasting while Jesus and His disciples are feasting.

The scribes are fasting while Jesus and His disciples are feasting. Wow! Jesus really likes a good party, huh?

They approach Jesus.

Question #3

Why don't your disciples act like we do?

Notice: They're confronting Jesus now, not about His actions, but about His followers. The progression continues what started within their hearts and moved to the fringes, until now they're confronting Him about His followers. Are you seeing the picture? Let's go to the fourth narrative and final why question.

It's the Sabbath controversy. You'll remember from our discussion in chapter five that the Sabbath was a time to cease, desist and remember. You'll also recall it had become everything, but that.

Rules. A lot of rules. And it seems Jesus and His disciples are disregarding them. Once again the religious elite are unhappy.

Confrontation.

Question #4

Why don't you obey our rules?

Again, notice the progression. They're in Jesus' face confronting Him.

Finally, the last narrative in our section. Jesus heals a man with a paralyzed hand. He literally gives this man his life back. On a day when the religious leadership should have been rejoicing for what God had done, should have been directing everyone with a need to the feet of Jesus, they stomp out and plot with the Herodians (the political leadership) about how they might *annihilate, destroy, assassinate* Jesus. It's out in the open. Their hearts are hardened.

> *On a day when the religious leadership should have been rejoicing for what God had done, they stomped out.*

Remember the progression:

It started in their hearts.

Worked its way to the fringes.

They confront Jesus about His followers.

They simply confront Jesus.

Then, they reject Him…want Him out of the picture.

They'll have it their way.

So?

Why is this important? Because eventually, the real *you* is going to show up. Who you are on the inside will be revealed. It's the whole tree and fruit thing.

From Billy:

I'm a city boy: I grew up in Cincinnati, went to college south of Chicago, lived in Chicagoland for a while, and then moved back to Cincinnati. In other words: I didn't grow up on the farm. I never even had a garden. But even I know that if I purchase an apple tree, take it home, and plant it in my back yard, and allow the seasons to change, I'll eventually see apples. If pears appear on the limbs, I know what I purchased really wasn't an apple tree.

Sooner or later what's on the inside will be revealed.

From their hearts, to the hardness of their hearts.

When we read about *heart*, it's important to realize that—in this context—we're not talking about sentimental, affectionate, romantic types of things. In Jewish thought process, the *heart* isn't emotional language. As mentioned earlier, their seat of emotions was considered their bowels! (This changes the tone of romantic conversation a bit, doesn't it?)

So when we refer to the heart—in this context—we're referring to the sum total of the individual. It's the inner self, the core of the person. It's what makes him him (or her her). It's who he IS.

And who are they? Upon what is their kingdom built?

Externals.

In fact you could call them externalists: They had a relationship with God based upon their activity and works. Whenever you have a religion built upon activity, it always leads to self-righteousness. If I can judge how close I am to God by the way I act, look, etc., then I can judge how close you are. It's the pat on the back and it feels good.

This is not what Jesus' kingdom is all about. Take a closer look at the canvas. Do you remember we mentioned that two kingdoms were about to collide? Well, Jesus was offering grace. That's very different. The scribes and Pharisees were very proud of their religiosity.

Jesus was constantly pointing to the Father. He was only concerned about God's approval.

Jesus was painting humility.

They were into external ceremony; Jesus was into a transformed heart.

They loved the approval of man.

If we whittle it down to the simplest of forms: They had their ritual, and Jesus was offering relationship.

Empty ritual is the enemy of authentic relationship.

They had their patterns and certainly observed their practices. But, in the midst of that, they missed the Person. They should have seen, but they missed Him. They'd rather have it their way.

Meaningless routine is not the same as meaningful relationship. Everything we do needs to be centered and focused on Him. The Person must dictate our patterns, not the other way around. Without Him, we're simply going through the motions. *May that never be.*

It All Comes Down To...

Do you realize the greatest struggle we will ever face will always be found right here? In our hearts.

At the core.

At the center.

This has always been the case.

It will always be true.

Need proof? This can be illustrated by returning to the beginning of the story. Not the story we're involved with in this chapter, but the story of all things. The story that's found in Genesis.

Your story.

My story.

Our story.

Do you remember the day the Creator God creates man, fills him with life, and places him in the garden He specifically designed for them? He spoke a word of freedom. Let's eavesdrop on the conversation.

"When I made this place, Adam, I had *you* in mind. I want you to live life to the fullest! Name the animals and frolic with them. Do you see the trees? All the colorful things hanging from the limbs? Eat them! You'll love the taste of the orange one! They're yours. Everything.

"Just stay away from the tree that's in the center of the garden. Don't eat of the one in the *center*, the tree of knowledge of good and evil, because when you eat of that one you'll die."

That's how it began.

From Billy:

I struggled with this for the longest time. I'm analytical. I'm logical and reasonable. I can't help it; It's simply how I'm wired, and this just didn't make sense. I thought: *Seriously? This is the plan? Come on God, You're smarter than this.* How do I know? Because even I'm smarter than that!

Think about it: If I didn't want you to eat from a tree, I know what I'd do. I'd put it on the heights of a remote mountain, because I know we're too lazy to climb to it. Or maybe I'd put it in the far east corner of the garden and hide it behind some bigger, more beautiful tree. I'd make it a prune tree. I certainly wouldn't put it in the center of their existence.

But, He did.

Right in the middle.

Right at the core.

Right in the center.

Then I realized: That's the spot He wants to occupy. Man was created for relationship. However, forced relationship is not relationship at all. Manipulated love is not love. There needed to be an expression of their love. Thus, the tree.

The Center. That's where He wants to be.

It will always be the source of our greatest struggle. It was Adam's battle. It was Eve's war. It was the scribes' struggle, and it's our fight as well.

What's at the core?
They missed Him.
They'd have it their way.
It's who they were.
What's at the center of *your* life?

Going Deeper

(To be answered individually or with a small group.)

- Identify a few things that have the potential of becoming rituals in your life.
- Have you ever thought about how deeply God longs to be in a proper relationship with you? Right in the center of who you are? How does that make you feel? How does it prompt you to respond?
- What are the things in your life that battle for control? What things define you? How does that affect your relationship with God? With others?
- Take an honest look at your relationship with Jesus. Is He the center of your life? If not, what changes would you need to make in order to put Him at the center? How would this affect your other relationships?

Prayer time: Lord, search me for anything that has replaced an authentic relationship with You. I don't want to be so caught up in my routines that I miss who You are. Be the center of my life.

CHAPTER
TWELVE

It costs a lot to live like Christ—to reach out to the poorest of the poor, to love the unlovable—to be the hands and feet for someone.
It takes time, energy and sometimes money.

It's hard.

Why would we do this?

Because He did it for us.

And because we want to become like Him.

So how far would you go to get a friend to Jesus?

ON THE MOVE

(Matthew 9:9; Mark 2:8-14)

"Why does He talk like this? Only God can forgive sins."

That's what they're saying.

The scribes and Pharisees—the religious leadership of the day—are in an uproar because of the statement Jesus has made. Their egos have been bruised! Remember, the people are saying Jesus teaches better than the professionals: the scribes and Pharisees. He teaches as one having authority, like He actually knows what He's talking about. These insecure, intimidated, religious leaders are now looking for any reason to discredit Him. In their hearts, they think they've got Him.

Have you noticed we can't get anything by Jesus? He's the Knower of our hearts. We simply *think* something and He knows. Jesus knows exactly what these guys are thinking!

Disagreeing

Jesus knew their hearts, but He could see on their faces they disagreed with His statement. He knows where they are, but He refuses to leave them there. Have you realized this about the Artist? He knows exactly where we are. He meets us there. But He refuses to leave us in that position. He's constantly working on His masterpiece—restoring it to what He knows it can be.

He knows exactly what these people are thinking, what's going on in their hearts, where they are, yet He refuses to leave them there. Listen as He speaks:

"Why do you reason about these things in your hearts?
Which is easier, to say to the paralytic, 'Your sins are forgiven you,'
or to say, 'Arise, take up your bed and walk'?"
(Mark 2:8-9 NKJV)

Let's think about this question for a minute.

How would you answer?

Before you do....which would be easier for the paralytic? Remember, his body doesn't work. There's no strength in his legs, no developed muscle. He's the unwelcome, unloved outcast. All eyes are on him.

How about the scribes? What would be easier for them to hear as they sit in judgment and condemnation?

What about the crowd?

Let's note that everyone is *not* at the same place in the story. We all come from somewhere, each has a perspective dictated by his or her circumstance; all have a point of view. It's too easy for us to quickly jump to conclusions and make judgments. How would you answer?

The story continues:

"'But that you may know that the Son of Man has power on earth
to forgive sins' —He said to the paralytic..."
(Mark 2:10 NKJV).

Excitement of the Miracle

Can you imagine the excitement of the four burden-bearers at this point? This is exactly why they brought their "burden" here. Their journey wasn't motivated by the concern for this man's sin. They brought the paralytic to Jesus for his physical paralysis to be healed.

First, Jesus would deal with the spiritual.

Now it was going to happen. They're around the hole they uncovered in the roof. They're dirty, bleeding, tired. But their efforts would pay off. Jesus was about to lift this burden. Imagine their anticipation as they begin to cheer Him on: "Yes! That's why we brought him here! Make him walk, make him walk!"

Jesus focuses upon the man on the mat and continues speaking.

> *"I say to you, arise, take up your bed, and go to your house"*
> *(Mark 2:11 NKJV).*

The entire crowd is engaged in the moment. Every eye is transfixed on the lifeless form that had been lowered through the roof. Suddenly, fingers that were motionless start to twitch.

Crooked legs begin to straighten.

Twisted, limp arms gather strength.

The picture mesmerizes the crowd as the new arms push up from the floor so he can try out his new legs. As he stands, he doesn't stumble once! As he stretches, squares his shoulders and lifts his head, we notice he stands as tall as anyone in the house. He looks over at the mat where he had been enslaved with the sentence he had lived with for so long.

As he stretches, squares his shoulders and lifts his head, we notice he stands as tall as anyone in the house.

He's going to claim that baggage. He leans over. There's a gasp as everyone sees—without stumbling—he bends over and grabs the mat. As he throws it over his shoulder, the entire crowd in the house parts. Yes, the same crowd who wouldn't let him in, now has no choice, but to make room for the walking miracle.

"Immediately he arose, took up the bed, and went out
in the presence of them all"
(Mark 2:12 NKJV).

He's walking out!

In full view of everyone.

This is not the same man.

Well, it *is* the same man.

Only, Jesus has transformed his life.

The Artist has restored His masterpiece!

Can you imagine being there? How would you have responded? Let's look at *their* response:

"...so that all were amazed and glorified God, saying,
'We never saw anything like this!'"
(Mark 2:12 NKJV)

Their jaws are on the ground. With their very eyes they saw it. A man lowered through the roof walked out in full view. Amazing. Stunning. Incredible. They're asking, "What in the world did we just see?"

Let's pause for a moment. It's time for a question: When was the last time you left a gathering saying, "What in the world...?" Not because something chaotic happened or a spectacle occurred, but because Jesus came upon the scene in such a real way that there was no other way to explain it. He was simply revealed and lives were changed! Don't you long for that?

So, when was it?

Has it been recently?

Or, have you *ever* experienced that?

Isn't that what we as Christians long for?

We want to see Him!

"We never saw anything like this!"

That's what they're saying.

Jesus changed a life.

In a very public way.

Simply amazing.

Now, He's on the move…again.

Familiarity

> *"Then He went out again by the sea"*
> (Mark 2:13 NKJV).

Let's look closely at this phrase. Jesus has just caused the paralytic to walk. It was a prodigious scene. Words couldn't really describe it. Now Jesus is on the move. We read that He goes out again.

Please don't read past the adverb *again*. It's a real temptation, isn't it? It's one of those words that are so simple and so common that we don't give it much consideration.

When we read that Jesus goes out *again* we understand that this is a journey He has made before. It's a path He's already traveled. And He'll do it again in the future. To be technical: Jesus departs from the house to go to a previous location for another time. He goes out *again*.

Where's He going?

By the sea.

What sea? It's the Sea of Galilee, the largest body of fresh water in this region. It's the sea where we saw the fisherman casting and drawing their nets. It's where He called

Jesus changed a life.
In a very public way.

them to follow Him into a life of responding and transformation. It's the sea where He spends two thirds of His earthly ministry: The Sea of Galilee.

Why's He going there?

Do you remember chapter seven of this book: "Disobedience Costs"? It was in that chapter when we were at the end of Mark 1 and we saw Jesus leaving Capernaum and going to the wilderness.

Jesus was proclaiming the Kingdom: The Kingdom was going public.

At that time, He was leaving to escape the commotion being caused by the disobedience of the transformed leper. Hysteria had risen to such a level that the crowds were getting caught up in the signs, wonders and healing. Jesus was proclaiming the Kingdom: The Kingdom was going public. The crowds were hindering the work, so He retreated.

That's not what's happening here. In fact, it's the exact opposite. Jesus leaves the house to go to a place He had been before: the sea. He's going to the sea not to escape the crowds. Rather, He's going to a place where He could accommodate them. The house had been much too confining. The walls had kept Jesus from being as effective as He could. The walls and the curious crowds had prevented those who needed to get to Jesus from reaching Him.

Jesus goes to a natural location He was familiar with and could be most effective. He goes to where He will be able to accommodate the crowds:

> "...and all the multitude came to Him, and He taught them"
> (Mark 2:13 NKJV).

All the multitude came to Him.

This is a fascinating picture.

There was still so much excitement about Jesus that when He leaves, they follow. Not only do they follow, but we can imagine that they gathered momentum as they went. What will be the response of the people who weren't at the house when they see a once-paralyzed man now running down the street? Certainly their curiosity is peaked! Not to mention the multitude walking toward the seashore. Is it a parade? Dignitary? What's happening? They gather there and Jesus teaches them.

No concert.

No frills.

No magic show or performance.

Jesus teaches them. He unveils the canvas.

And Again...

When the teaching time is over, Jesus is on the move again. He seems to have something in mind. There's an appointment He must keep. Where He's headed, we really don't know. Is He going back to the house? He's a carpenter and there's a hole in the roof that requires repair. Who knows? Or, perhaps, He needs to go to market. Maybe He's simply going for a stroll. Here's what we read:

"As Jesus went on from there, he saw a man named Matthew sitting at the tax collector's booth"
(Matthew 9:9 NIV).

This is such a simple statement and yet in its simplicity, we encounter the profound. It's a beautiful statement because it reveals glorious truth. If we're not careful we'll read it too quickly and miss it.

Let's stay here for a while and allow this reality to penetrate our hearts.
Let's look a little closer.

"...He saw Matthew..."

He saw. To really understand this statement we're going to need
to return to the house where Jesus was interrupted by the four men
tearing the hole in the roof. Do you remember what it said about Jesus?

"When Jesus saw their faith..."
(Mark 2:5 NKJV).

It's the same word that's used here. Why is this significant?
Think about this: If we're simply to understand it as a physical sight
type of deal, it wouldn't have been hard to see. They tore a hole in
the roof! If they didn't believe Jesus could do something about the
man's condition, they wouldn't have gone as far as to do something so
improper.

It's deeper than physical sight.

This is illustrated when Jesus sees beyond the exterior of the
paralytic and addresses the complete person.

Digging Deeper

Let's look into it like this: It's the Greek word *eidon*, from the
root *eidó* (pronounced i'-do), and it carries with it the meaning of sight.
Physical sight, yes. But it goes so much deeper than that. It's more
properly understood as perception--to perceive, to be aware, to notice,
to discover, to have regard for, to cherish, pay attention to, to discern.

Wow.

Do you see how that changes the picture?

Jesus perceived Matthew.

Jesus was aware of Matthew.

Jesus noticed Matthew.

Jesus had regard for Matthew.

Jesus paid attention to Matthew.

Jesus cherished Matthew.

Don't let the gravity of this statement slip by unnoticed. Remember where they are—by the Sea of Galilee. There's a lot of activity here.

Fishermen are at the sea counting their fish.

Some are mending their nets.

Boats are arriving and departing.

We see travelers. We notice taxpayers.

This is a hub for commerce. Buyers and sellers are busy here.

Somehow in the midst of all the people, all the activity, Jesus was aware of Matthew. He noticed the tax collector. He paid attention to the son of Alpheus. The language is very specific. It doesn't say He saw people, activity or crowds. No. *He cherished Matthew.*

He was in pursuit of His masterpiece.

It's almost as though this was the motivation behind His movement today. He was in pursuit of His masterpiece.

Such a contrast. Before, four men brought one to Jesus who couldn't bring himself. Now, we see Jesus going to one who would never bring himself to Jesus. Why? Because He saw him.

Let's pray that we comprehend a bit of the magnitude of that statement.

Noticing. Cherishing.

It's so amazing. Why? Because it's so easy not to see, to not be aware, to not notice, pay attention, have regard for, or cherish. We live life unto ourselves.

From Billy:

It was 1994. I was a senior religion major preparing for ministry. As a senior, I was required to spend the last eight weeks of my final semester involved in an internship. They called it "field placement" because the student would be placed in a church and spend eight weeks away from campus to discover what it meant to serve in the capacity of a local church. It was to prepare the student for pastoral ministry.

Here's the thing: I've never felt called to pastoral ministry. That's just not me or my gifting. I tried everything I could to get out of going. Short from dropping out, I had no choice. So, I went.

I was sent to a church in Crown Point, Ind. It was a great church with a wonderful pastor, staff and people. I'll admit, it was exciting to be a part of what God was doing there.

I was offered the youth pastor position and accepted. It was thrilling to watch as a handful of teenagers got excited about Jesus and began to change the world. The program grew, and I was in over my head. But what a feeling! I will always be thankful for that time.

One Sunday morning I was going through my normal routine. I had an adult youth staff of about 25 that made sure that the program ran smoothly: Sunday school classes, leadership teams, etc. I had a habit of making sure everything was going the way it was supposed to, so I was checking things out in the youth center. I had something else on my mind, however that I needed to take care of before worship that morning.

I started through the hallways, passed the offices, entered the building where the sanctuary was, rounded the corner to the foyer when at that point I almost plowed a woman down. I was consumed in thought and almost ran right over her.

Encounter

I'm glad I didn't. It was one of my teenager's parents and she was looking for me. I could tell something concerned her when she said sternly, "Billy, I need to talk to you!"

I suspected this was a conversation best not held in the foyer of the church before Sunday morning worship. So we went back to the office area. There were some shared work spaces that would be a perfect semi-private location to speak. When we reached one of those areas, the conversation continued. I'll never forget her voice as she asked, "Billy, I need to know something: Why don't you like me?"

Understand this please: I didn't *not* like her. I really didn't know where that was coming from until now. You see, I didn't feel anything toward her. I never took the time to see what was going on with her or her daughter. Her daughter wasn't on my leadership team, wasn't a stand-out student, and I guess I just assumed some of the other adults were taking the time. I had never taken the time to see. I'm thankful for a confrontation in a warm foyer on a cold day in Northwest Indiana, when I was made aware of my lack of warmth, my coldness to those around me.

We live life unto ourselves. We see physically, but we don't perceive. We get consumed in so many other things we don't take the time to be aware of others with whom we're not consumed. We lack regard for our fellow man. We simply don't pay attention.

Always Perceiving

Jesus does.

You know those times when you feel terribly alone and your heart is shattering into a million pieces? Think no one sees?

Jesus notices.

How about those times when you have to go to school or work and you simply feel invisible? Does anyone care?

Jesus is aware.

Overlooked?

Jesus pays attention.

Feel as though no one cares?

Jesus cherishes.

This is what's so beautiful: Just as Jesus saw Levi, He sees you. You're the reason He took the path He did. You were on His mind.

He saw Matthew. He sees You.

In a world filled with billions of people,

He notices you.

    He is aware of you.

        He cherishes you.

           You're His motivation.

              You're His masterpiece.

Never forget.

Going Deeper

(To be answered individually or with a small group.)

- What are some of the issues that develop from becoming too absorbed with what's happening in our individual lives?
- Have you ever felt as though people didn't really see you? Have you ever known someone whom everyone else seems to look right past? How should we respond to these feelings? These people?
- Describe a few people in your life whom you really, truly, genuinely, wholeheartedly love? How does it feel to know that the Master Artist feels this way about you—times infinity?

Prayer time: Dear Jesus, I love You. Thank You for loving and cherishing me. Sometimes I'm so overwhelmed by Your love, it's hard to believe. Thank You for loving me unconditionally! I realize that You were motivated by me to do what You've done to express that love. Help me not just to be thankful, but help me to be determined to be a vessel to those around me who know nothing of Your love. Open my eyes as You open my heart to the world around me. Help me never take Your love for granted.

CHAPTER
THIRTEEN

Have you ever felt unworthy—as though God can't use you?
If so, you can relate to Matthew.
He was in a less-than-ideal vocation, but Christ saw his
potential.
He knew what Matthew could become.
Christ sees the possibilities in you as well.
He dreams big for you.

When the Master Artist invites you inside the canvas, it's for
eternity.

NO PLAN B

(Matthew 9:9; Mark 2:13-14)

From Billy:

Third grade is a wonderful time in a child's life. It's that time when little boys begin to notice little girls; when they begin to realize there's something different about them, something wonderful. They begin to try to get their attention by pulling their hair and punching them in the arm. You know, to show them how special they are. It's how little boys express themselves.

It was certainly a memorable time in my life.

I was a student at Williams Avenue Elementary. As a little boy, I was now beginning to notice girls. Not the girls my age. Instead, I had my eye on a greater prize: Miss Parsons, the music teacher. She was smart. She was talented. She was kind. And, to top it off, she was beautiful. Childhood crush...she was my kind of woman!

Rhonda's story was different. Because, well, Rhonda was different.

Rhonda lived around the block from me and was in my third grade class. She came from a home where life was anything but easy. Mom and Dad lived their lives without much regard for her. Or at least that's how it seemed. She was heavier than the rest of us and wasn't taught much about personal hygiene. She didn't have the nicest of clothes and often whatever she wore on Monday she would still be wearing on Friday. Needless to say, we noticed, and we let her know how different she was. Children can be cruel.

Life can be tough when you're different. Life was tough for Rhonda.

Not only did Miss Parsons notice, she cared.

We often had activities in music class that required a partner. Whether it was sharing an autoharp, dancing, or singing a duet in our choir, the Melody Makers, we'd have to partner off. Sometimes those partners were assigned, other times we'd choose.

All the boys would line up against one wall and the girls on the other. From the first boy to the last, partners would be chosen. It was a process that could be exhilarating. If you were in the front of the line you had the pick of the litter. It was a process that could be excruciating: If you were at the end of the line you were stuck with whoever wasn't chosen. Rhonda was always that one not chosen.

Her body language began to tell the story. Whenever it was time to partner off, she'd take her place with the other girls. She'd stand at the end of the line with her shoulders slumped, head down, realizing she was going to hear Miss Parsons force the last boy to be her partner.

I can't imagine how that felt. Sure, there were plenty of times I wasn't first choice and I know at least once or twice I was chosen last. But every time? I can't begin to understand what that would have done for one's self image at such a young age. Unwanted. Overlooked. Last choice. Rhonda.

A Shocking Turn of Events

I was helping Miss Parsons between classes one day. (I always found a reason to be around Miss Parsons.) As I began to wrap things up so I could get to my class, she asked me to do her a favor. Of course! I'd do anything she wanted me to do! But I wasn't ready for what she said:

"Next time we have a partner time in class, I want you to pick Rhonda to be your partner. Will you do that?"

I couldn't believe my ears. Didn't she know what she was asking of me? This is the third grade. Little boys and girls are beginning to notice each other. If I partner with Rhonda that will be the end! How could such an ugly request come from such a beautiful mouth? No way, no thanks; I'd never do that. I didn't really care for Miss Parsons anymore.

I turned to storm out of the room as she continued, "Billy, it's what a Christian would do."

I knew she was right. She knew I knew. I came from a church-going family. But, to be honest, I didn't care.

Time passed. I don't know how long. Eventually it was time. We had a partner activity in music class. Miss Parsons lined all the girls up along the wall. Rhonda took her place at the end of the line, head down, shoulders slumped. Then she lined the boys up along the opposite wall. And, for some reason, today was my lucky day. I was right in the front. I was first. I'd have first choice.

I heard her voice, "Billy, pick your partner."

My heart was pounding as I looked up and down the line. I saw Lisa, Lori and Lana. I saw all the girls whom I wanted to choose as my partner and was trying to figure out whose day I was going to make.

Then I saw Rhonda.

Head down, shoulders slumped and my heart began to pound faster. So, I made my choice:

"Rhonda."

He was despised. Detested.

When people glanced his way, it was usually with disdain.

He was the lowest of the low. He was numbered with thieves, murderers and rapists. His touch would render your household unclean just as that of the leper. At least the leper had no control over his circumstance. But *this* was his choice.

He was the lowest of the low. He was numbered with thieves, murderers and rapists.

He had traded away his family — mother, father, brother, and sister. Why? For monetary gain. He was driven by the desire for wealth and he had no familial concern.

He walked away from his people. A traitor to his fellow Jews. He served the hand of their oppressor. He had no societal concern.

By walking away from his people, he'd turned his back on his God. That's why he wasn't welcomed by the religious leadership. That's why they'd say you could lie to him with no fear of punishment. He was numbered with the sinners. Actually, lower than a sinner himself. It's how it's listed in scripture, "tax collectors and sinners." He had no religious concern.

He was a person of the dirt.

Treasonous. Extortioner.

He had the stench of greed. Money was his oxygen.

He was the tax collector.

Yet, this was the one whom Jesus pursued.

This was the one whom Jesus saw.

This was the one whom Jesus chose. The one whom Jesus called.

"As Jesus went on from there, he saw a man named Matthew sitting at the tax collector's booth. 'Follow me,' he told him"
(Matthew 9:9 NIV).

The Artist uses two types of invitations to call us onto the canvas. We've already heard Him call the disciples. Now we'll see Him invite a tax collector—one who most would say shouldn't be included in the painting. While there are some similarities in the two invitations, there are also some important differences. Let's look a little closer.

They catch fish for a living, not to hang on the wall in their den, or family room above the fireplace.

First, let's look at *whom* He calls. We talked about it in chapter four of this book. This is the day Jesus is walking along the Sea of Galilee and sees some fishermen. They catch fish for a living, not to hang on the wall in their den or family room above the fireplace. It was their livelihood. Cast the net. Draw the net. These are the men whom Jesus stands before and calls to a new life of attachment to Him.

Who Are They?

They're the religious crowd. These are the men who grew up in the right home. They were raised in Synagogue. They had been trained. They believed their training. How can I say that? Remember, they were looking for a Messiah. They believed their God was going to send a Deliverer. They had lived under the tyranny of Rome long enough. There would be a renewed exodus, and they'd have a land of their own like God promised.

We know Andrew, at least, had attached himself to John the Baptist: You know, that strange man, in a strange dwelling, with a strange dress, eating a strange diet, with a strange response. In John 1:41-42 he goes to Simon and says that Jesus is the One they've been looking for, the Messiah, the Christ. In other words, they were the religious bunch, the church crowd.

Back to Matthew

Who is he? This is the one who has sold his soul to the non-Jews, the Gentiles, the Romans. He was in league with the unclean and the idolaters. The betrayer, extortioner, outcast, greedy...think of any derogatory adjective you can come up with and that's him. The one with no spiritual concern. In other words, the irreligious. It seems he couldn't care less about his God. He had traded it all away. That's *who* He called.

Can you see the difference?

Secondly, let's examine *how* He called. This is where the stories become highly intriguing.

Go back to the calling of the fishermen, the religious crowd.

Listen to what Jesus says:

"Follow Me, and I will make you become fishers of men."

Let's slow down and re-examine this statement.

Jesus stands before these men and commands, "Follow Me." But notice He doesn't stop there. He goes on, "and I will make you... to become." You could say on this occasion Jesus gives an if/then statement. If you follow me, then I will make you...to become. He gives the command and then qualifies the command with a promise. There's something in it for them. Jesus would do a work. He would make them into what He wanted them to become. That's how He called the religious.

He gives the command and then qualifies the command with a promise.

Now, look at Matthew.

Jesus seeks Him out, just as He had the fishermen. Jesus is the

One who stops before him, again, just as He had the fisherman. And, He speaks:

"Follow Me."

That's it. That's all He says. This is much different than with the fishermen. There's the command—the imperative to follow. It's an interruption of how things have been; a command to step out of an old world into a new. However, there's no qualifier, no promise

Jesus doesn't say to this man of the world, "Follow Me and all your dreams will come true," or "Follow Me and you'll never lack for anything." He doesn't even promise to make him into what He wants him to be. Simply: Follow—without any promise of provision. That's how He called Matthew, the tax collector, the scum, the irreligious.

Does this seem backward?

If anyone needed a promise to persuade him to follow Jesus, wouldn't it be the unconcerned, the irreligious? Bring it into our context. We who are part of His church shouldn't need if/then statements. "If you follow Jesus, then He'll…" or "Love Jesus and you'll get…" For those of us who know Him, that should be enough!

Look at Jesus. Look into His face. How can you not love Him? How can you not follow? It's the world, the unchurched, the unconcerned who should need the persuading. Not the other way around.

We can be glad God doesn't do things the way we would. He always knows exactly what He's doing.

When He calls the fishermen, He commands and promises. To Matthew, however, He simply gives the command. Now Matthew would respond. Either he'd demand tax, or he'd get up and follow. One way or another, there would be a response.

This is probably a good place for a reminder: When Jesus speaks, it demands an immediate response. Determined by that response, we will never be the same again. The Artist is at work. He knows what He's doing. Do we trust Him enough to respond to the strokes of His brush whether or not we understand?

How does Matthew respond?

> *"...and Matthew got up and followed him"*
> *(Matthew 9:9 NIV).*

The Drama Thickens

We have Matthew, a man of the world, unconcerned, no religion, no social standing, being called to step into a new world. This world was completely different from the one he knew. His world was one controlled by greed. It's what he lived for, why he got out of bed in the morning. So, you can only imagine the type of personality he had. The concerns. The discussions. The what if's.

How would you respond to Jesus' command? Would you make a list of pros and cons? Or would you initiate a discussion regarding opportunities for advancement? Perhaps you'd ask about a salary package, benefits or what color the carpet is in the parsonage. Isn't that how things are done? There are questions that need to be answered, plans that need to be made, details that must be tended to.

How would you respond to Jesus' command? Would you make a list of pros and cons?

Not Matthew.

There must have been something about the way Jesus said it; the passion in His voice or the authority in His words.

Or maybe it was the look in His eyes.

Perhaps Matthew just realized his need.

When Jesus spoke, we get the sense that without any hesitation Matthew pushes back from the tax desk. The sound of the wooden chair skipping across the ground is a proclamation that there's going to be a change. Coins are dropped. What he had traded everything for is now left in the dust. He had a new desire, a new object of affection, a new Master—Jesus Christ.

How is it different from the response of the fishermen?

Simply put: You can always go back to fishing. The fish are going to be there for anybody who will cast a net into the sea. There will always be a spot for a seasoned fisherman. And let's face it, Simon and Andrew, James and John, owned the business. The boats were theirs. The nets belonged to them.

Their natural response when things didn't turn out the way they thought it should—didn't happen just the way they planned—was to get back in the boats, grab their nets and fish. You can always go back to fishing. There was always a plan B.

You'll never go back to the tax office.

Matthew was the low man on the totem pole in the tax structure of the day. He had purchased the rights to sit at that spot and collect tax. So you can be sure as soon as there was a vacancy it would be sold to the highest bidder. There were other people of the dirt willing to trade everything for wealth. There would be no turning back. The cost would require all. And Matthew was willing to pay.

No turning back. No plan B.

From Billy:

"Rhonda."

I looked and Rhonda just stood there; head down,

shoulders slumped.

I thought maybe I didn't say it loud enough so I took a deep breath and once again spoke, "Rhonda."

Still no response! At this point I'm becoming a little offended. I've not only chosen Rhonda once, but twice, and she hasn't responded! She hasn't even acknowledged me. Oh, everybody else was responding: The guys next to me began to punch me in the arm and laugh. I could see that even some of the girls were beginning to snicker. But there was nothing I could do now. Everyone had heard. Well, everyone except for Rhonda. I took a deeper breath and spoke in a louder voice:

"Rhonda."

I'll never forget what happened next.

I watched as slowly, Rhonda began to lift her head. I noticed something on her face I can't remember ever seeing before. She wore the brightest, biggest, most beautiful smile I ever saw. She began to square her shoulders and held her head high as she walked to meet me in the center of the room. Not because I was the one; I know there were girls that wouldn't have wanted to dance with me. It was just now, for once in her life, Rhonda was someone special! She hadn't been looked over. She wasn't forced upon someone. She was somebody.

Do you realize how special you are to Jesus? It's all about you!

Are you looking at the canvas? Do you see Jesus, the Master Artist? He's standing on the edge of time looking at you. Maybe you don't seem to have much to offer or perhaps others have claimed you have no value, but He sees you as His masterpiece. He loves you so much He'll do whatever it will take to restore what He has created you to be. Even giving His life.

He came. He pursued. He called.

Motivated by love: A dream in His heart.

What's the proper response to such love?

All.

No turning back.

No plan B.

Going Deeper

(To be answered individually or with a small group.)

- Can you relate to the opening story about Rhonda? Have you known a Rhonda? Or have you felt like Rhonda?
- Describe what it felt like when you truly began to realize how special you are to Christ. Right now, how does it make you feel to realize it really IS all about *you?*
- Who do you know that needs to be told how special he or she is to Jesus? How can you get that message to them this week?
- Have you left the tax booth? Fishing boats, nets? Or, do you have a plan B?

Prayer time: Jesus, it's overwhelming to know that you chose me! I'm so thankful. Help me to live knowing how special I am to You, that You were motivated by me! Thank You! I really long to follow You completely, without any plan B. If there are other things I'm trusting in or holding onto, reveal them to me so I can commit them to You. I don't have much to offer, but I have me. I want to be wholly Yours.

CHAPTER
FOURTEEN

Gale-force winds.

Lightning strong enough to split a boat.

We tend to focus on the storm.

But the Master Artist is still focused on you.

This, however, is where *your* focus shifts.

Christ's attributes are beginning to take shape in you.

His thoughts and views and actions are becoming yours.

As you focus on Him through total surrender, He shapes you in
His image.

WHEN STORMS COME

(Mark 4:35-41; 6:45-53)

There's something wonderful about a good storm; the mighty rolls of thunder, majestic flashes of lightening and the metered pitter patter of raindrops sometimes gentle, other times fierce. It's an incredible display matched by few others.

From Billy:

I've always loved a good storm. I can remember as a boy sitting on the porch in southwestern Ohio with my dad simply listening, observing, feeling the storm as it came and went. I can even remember one time when half our city block was being rained on while the other half was dry and sunny. There's no other way to say it: Simply amazing!

When I moved to northeast Illinois for college I experienced storms in a whole new way. The Ohio Valley is filled with rolling hills that eventually grow into the Appalachian Mountains. Northeast Illinois is flat; you can see for miles. I remember times when the wind would pick up and you could literally watch the storm brew and advance across the horizon.

I can't help it; I just love a good storm.

But not all storms are good.

We've all seen reports of the devastation left behind the path of a tornado, hurricane or tsunami. Homes demolished. Cities wiped out.

Landscapes forever changed. Lives stolen. Certainly, not all storms are good.

Just as we have seasons in our lives, we will also experience storms. Henry Wadsworth Longfellow stated this reality when he penned the words, "Into each life some rain must fall."

There's simply no way around it. Storms are a part of life. Some we'll see brewing on the horizon. Others will blow in unaware. In a moment we find ourselves in a situation that we seem to be clinging for our lives. We wonder if our homes will withstand the gust, how or if we'll make it through, and dread to see the changed landscape when the sun shatters the darkness.

What do we do in those times?

How should we respond?

Take courage. It's still all about you.

Get Ready

In Mark 4:35-41 and Mark 6:45-53 we learn some powerful lessons on what to do when storms come. There are two recorded physical storms in the disciples' walk with Jesus. Undoubtedly, there were more than just two storms in the three years they were together, but these two must be significant because we have their account in Scripture. Both happened during the second year of their walk with Jesus and both occurred while they were in a boat on the sea.

Water was, is, and always will be, of great importance to any culture.

Water was, is, and always will be, of great importance to any culture. In Scripture, you see almost every major biblical event occurs near some water source. Throughout the Old Testament large bodies of water are synonymous with death. It had also been referred to as "the abyss."

Why? In biblical times they didn't have the technology we have. They weren't able to go far below the surface of the water and see what was beneath. They watched as people would venture out on the sea and never return. They heard the tales that had been spun from such events.

We've talked about the Sea of Galilee. You'll remember it's the largest body of fresh water in that region. It's a place of activity: commerce, travel and gathering. This sea was notorious. Because of the geography (from the air it would look like a basin of water surrounded by a mountain range) the mood of the sea could shift without warning. A stiff breeze could race down from the mountains and across the waters, changing smooth sailing into a nightmare for any traveler. This is the sea where these storms occur.

Kingdom Business

The Master Artist has been displaying the canvas. The Kingdom is growing. In fact, so many gathered to hear Him that today He actually taught from a boat. The day had been full, the crowds had been demanding.

When evening came and the teaching time was over, we hear Jesus speak to the disciples in a tired voice:

"Let us cross over to the other side"
(Mark 4:35 NKJV).

The disciples had also put in the exciting, but long hours of ministry. Longing for respite, they push out on the sea. As the boat sails from the shore, the crowds that gathered begin to disperse. The farther the boat gets from land, the crowds appear smaller and smaller until eventually they're out of the disciples' sight.

Turn of Events

Daylight gives way to night as they set their course. Jesus, tired from the demands of the day, makes His way to the back of the ship. He finds a cushion and lies down. The gentle breeze and rocking of the waves are perfect ingredients for much needed rest. He drifts into slumber.

The disciples scatter around the boat. They were enjoying the solitude, the peace, the rhythm of the sea.

With a fierce crash of thunder, the sky opens and begins to discharge its fury.

As the journey continues, the wind begins to strengthen. As the wind begins to challenge the ship, lightening fills the air. With a fierce crash of thunder, the sky opens and begins to discharge its fury. The gentle breeze is now ferocious and relaxing waves have become relentless—crashing into the boat.

The Battle Rages

The disciples are fighting. Jesus is asleep.

This is almost more than the disciples can take. Doesn't He realize what's going on? How can He sleep through this storm? How is that even possible? Enough! Something has to be done.

One of the disciples makes his way to the back of the boat. He's had all he can take. He walks over to where the cushion is and begins to shake it. We hear the fear, the concern, in his voice as he speaks:

"Teacher, do You not care that we are perishing?"
(Mark 4:38 NKJV)

We can translate this: "Jesus, the boat's filling up. We're losing the battle. Do something!" He's afraid for his life. Jesus understands.

We watch Jesus as He wipes the sleep from His eyes and stands. He makes His way to the front of the boat. He faces the tempest, looks it in the eye, and speaks:

"Peace, be still!"
(Mark 4:39 NKJV)

Jesus speaks, "Be muzzled."

When the word came from His mouth, as the last syllable flipped from His tongue, the storm must obey. The source of Authority has spoken.

The disciples are left wet, shivering and staring at each other.

Just as quickly as the mood of the sea shifted earlier, now it responds to the Master's voice. The winds die down. Stars reappear. It's smooth sailing for the rest of this journey. The disciples are left wet, shivering and staring at each other saying:

"Who can this be, that even the wind and the sea obey Him!"
(Mark 4:41 NKJV)

It's not really about weather, you know.
 Electric lightning that splits boats,
  gale-force winds that hurl boats,
   44-foot waves that sink boats.
It's not about the weather at all.
It's still about you.
Can you learn that even in the midst of your darkest night —
  your worst storm —
   your unimaginable nightmare —

that the Master Artist is at work?

He may be silent. You may not hear His voice right away.

But He's working behind the scenes in ways you can't see.

The doctor's office calls and the test results are back.

The news isn't good.

Your Savior knows all about it.

It seems you've had the children in church all their lives.

But now you're hearing rumors about your high-school daughter.

STDs?

Your Savior isn't shaken.

You promised "till death do us part."

But can you forgive yet another affair?

Your Savior has the answer.

You're a good person. But suddenly you find yourself in the midst of a storm. And it's not just any storm. Lightning has disintegrated the walls of your home. Your safe haven is now anything but.

Gale-force winds have hurled you into such pain you don't see how you'll regain balance. You're debilitated.

Your Savior isn't shaken. Your Savior has the answer.

The monstrous waves have beaten you prostrate into the darkness. You're wondering if you'll even recognize the sun should you ever see it again.

The answer is in the Master Artist. Though He may be silent, He is at work. He is moving, doing, restoring.

In the Greek language — the language in which the New Testament was originally written — there are two words for our "do." One is *prosso* and it's equated to an external activity. The disciples wanted Jesus to do something externally in the midst of the storm.

"Can You grab a bucket, Jesus? Will You help us? We need You!"

Prosso is physical activity. It's *engaging* oneself in physical activity.

The other word for "do" is *poieo.* Our word poetry is derived from this. It also refers to external activity—but it's strength that flows from the inside. It comes naturally.

As the Master Artist, He spreads His brush freely, with urgency and extreme focus, across the canvas of our lives. The beauty He creates in your life comes from within Him.

You are not simply on His "to DO" list; something to check off and accomplish externally. You are His "DOING"—His healing, restoring, beautifying, and *that* kind of "do" comes from deep within Himself. Out of *who He is,* He makes your life better.

From naturally within Him, He muzzles the wind.

He commands peace for your soul.

He stops the storm.

He draws you near.

It feels as though the focus is on the storm, doesn't it?

That's where our attention naturally goes.

But look closer. Perhaps in the lower deck, with His head on a pillow, you'll see the Master Artist who at any moment is about to poieo.

Can you trust Him? In the midst of a storm, can you trust Him? His focus isn't a storm. His focus is you.

A Miraculous Day

The entire day will be remembered forever. The Bible tells us five thousand people had been fed, but that's only counting the men. If we counted everyone, it would easily amount to ten or fifteen thousand. Women and children were there, too.

SUSIE SHELLENBERGER | BILLY HUDDLESTON

And how were they fed? Not by the caterers. Jesus did it with just a few fish and loaves. The crowds were ready to crown Him king.

The political climate seems delicate. John the Baptist has already been executed. The enemies of Jesus and the Kingdom were on the prowl; the Pharisees and Sadducees were in wait ready to pounce.

Jesus was aware.

> "Immediately He made His disciples get into the boat and go before Him to the other side, to Bethsaida, while He sent the multitude away"
> (Mark 6:45 NKJV).

Another Storm

We can hear His voice: "You go on to Bethsaida. I'll catch up with you later." The disciples are more than willing to do as Jesus said. The day had been exciting, but exhausting. We watch as they climb into the boat, press from the shore of the sea and begin to sail toward Bethsaida.

The day had been exciting, but exhausting.

As they do, Jesus makes His way to a mountain to pray. He would use this time to gather strength from His Father, direction for the storm He'd soon face. As He prays, the disciples sail.

Back in the boat, we watch as the sun has gone down. Once again, the disciples are in the midst of a storm. The wind picks up. Waves crash in. They spring into action; They fight the fight.

There's a big difference in this storm and the one they just survived in Mark 4. In the last storm Jesus was asleep in the back of the boat. Today, He's nowhere to be found. The One who had muzzled the storm was far from them. This would be it. They'd go down. This would be the end.

Can you imagine what they were feeling? Can you sense their confidence was nowhere to be found? What now? Notice the Scripture:

"Now when evening came, the boat was in the middle of the sea; and He was alone on the land. Then He saw them straining at rowing, for the wind was against them"
(Mark 6:48 NKJV).

That's probably the best description of how they were feeling: the wind was against them. Have you ever felt like that? One step forward, two steps back.

The oars are growing heavy. Their hands are rope-burned, backs are sore. For more than eight hours we get the sense they only made about three-and-a-half miles. They're barely holding their ground. They're about to go under. But, wait:

"Now about the fourth watch of the night He came to them, walking on the sea..."
(Mark 4:48 NKJV).

He came to them...walking on the sea. Think about this: A storm the disciples could not navigate or sail, Jesus walks right through. The wind cannot halt His movement. He gets in the boat with them, the wind dies down, and they anchor in Gennesaret.

We read about two storms during the disciples' time with Christ. Why does that matter to us? Because storms are a part of life. Sometimes we too, feel like crying out to the Artist, "I'm drowning! Don't You care? Are You even aware? Are You even here?"

Because to quote Wadsworth again: "It's inevitable that 'into each life some rain must fall.'" We need to be prepared. We want to know how to respond to the storms. We want to learn the lessons the disciples learned those nights. Here are five.

Lessons Learned

#1: Obedience doesn't equal ease. In each situation the disciples were simply doing what Jesus told them to do. They could have easily shouted, "Hey, Jesus! We're being obedient. So why are we in a storm? I mean, we're doing what You told us to do!"

Obedience doesn't equal ease. Read any book on persecuted Christians. Their obedience never equaled an easy life. (We recommend *In the Presence of My Enemies* by Gracia Burnham with Dean Merrill; *Heavenly Man* by Brother Yun; *Captive in Iran* by Maryam Rostampour and *Tortured for Christ* by Richard Wurmbrand.)

Obedience doesn't equal ease.

From Billy:

I was born in 1972, so that means I'm a product of the 80s. Those were my formative years. In the early part of that decade, my dad had an 80s van—sloped nose front, custom paint stripes down the side, tear drop tinted windows—slide the door open and shag carpet was everywhere. He thought he was cool! So did my friends and I.

We loved it when he gave us a ride to and from school in the cool van. We'd stop at Burger Chef and get milkshakes. The only problem? Well, music-wise dad was stuck in the 70s. He had an eight-track player in the van. (An eight-track player was like a CD player only totally different. I think cavemen invented it. It was used before cassette tape players were installed in cars. And I think those were invented by the early Romans.)

There was one song in particular I remember. The intro was vibrant as the artist began to sing, "I beg your pardon, I never promised you a rose garden!"

He never said it would be easy, but He said He'd be with us through it all. You know what that means? It's going to be good.

Jesus sees you in the storms. He's not ignorant to your situation.

Like the three Hebrew boys from the Old Testament who were thrown into the fiery furnace, "God will either save us from the flames, or He'll take us to heaven. Either way, He has our back." It will end well.

#2: **Don't quit.** The disciples learned this lesson right in the middle of the storm. Have you noticed the temptation to quit is always strong? When the storm is raging and the night is so dark it's hard to sense His presence, it would be easier to curl up in the fetal position and just give up. We've all been there.

Jesus sees you in the storms. He's not ignorant to your situation. Listen to the words of the psalmist in Psalm 121:1-4 NKJV:

I will lift up my eyes to the hills —
From whence comes my help?
My help comes from the Lord,
Who made heaven and earth.
He will not allow your foot to be moved;
He who keeps you will not slumber.

Behold, He who keeps Israel
Shall neither slumber nor sleep.

Don't quit. When you can't see Him, He never takes His eyes off you. He will not let you drown. He'll always come through. Which leads us to the third lesson.

#3: In the midst of your greatest need, He's there. Jesus went to the disciples. Moved by their circumstance, *He did not leave them on their own.* But when did He show up?

It wasn't when the storm began brewing.

Not even when the boat was half-full of water.

Jesus arrived when they needed Him most. When they saw no way out, He became their way out. They had reached the end of their striving and Jesus was there.

He's there. Wouldn't it be great to simply marinate in this truth for a while? So often we're tempted to do it on our own. So many times we think the answer lies in our efforts. And in the midst of our striving, we fail to realize He's there.

In every circumstance, He's there.

In the midst of every storm, He's there.

In the midst of your greatest need.

You are His masterpiece. Every stroke of the brush is restoring who you were meant to be. When situations are out of control...when the world is spinning wildly, chaotically, remember He's there because He cares. You are a dream in the Artist's heart. Each shade, every hue, is for your good. He is the Master. He's in control.

Jesus arrived when they needed Him most.

#4: You don't always end up where you thought you'd be. In Mark 6, Jesus told the disciples to go to Bethsaida and He'd catch up. However, after they struggled through the storm and Jesus got into the boat, they anchored in Gennesaret. (See Mark 6:53)

Gennesaret. That's not where they thought they were going. That wasn't on their itinerary; it wasn't a planned destination. Yet, that's where they ended up.

You don't always end up where you thought you'd be...but when Jesus is with you, it becomes the right place.

You know through the life you've lived thus far, that things don't always turn out the way you planned. Just talk to the young widow who lost her spouse to war and is left to raise a family on her own.

Speak with the father and mother whose son battled brain cancer at the age of 14. Then rejoiced at 15 because the battle seemingly had been won, cancer defeated. Yet it reared its ugly head more fiercely at 17 and claimed victory before his 18th birthday.

Sit down with the widower who lost his mate of 67 years and now lives life alone, losing part of who he is. They'd say, "It wasn't supposed to happen this way."

"We were going to grow old together."

"You're not supposed to outlive your child."

You don't always end up where you thought you'd be...but when Jesus is with you, it becomes the right place.

#5: You always land where you're needed most. You may not understand why you are where you are, but be sure of this: God will use you for His glory exactly where you stand.

The subheading in the *New King James Bible* to Mark 6:53-56 (when they anchor in Gennesaret) says this: **Many Touch Him and Are Made Well**

It seems odd to highlight a subheading, but it's important we catch it: **MANY**. Because they anchored there, *many* lives were changed. It's not where they thought they were going. But it's exactly where they needed to be. People were changed, lives transformed, masterpieces restored by the Master Artist Himself.

Turbulence Happened

Two storms in the disciples' three years with Jesus. In the first, Jesus was present. He was asleep in the stern. In the second, He had withdrawn to a mountain while the disciples struggled. The darkness of night prevented them from seeing Him, but He could see them.

The difference is great.

The withdrawal was necessary.

Why? Because Jesus knew the disciples would soon be in the storm of their lives. They needed to learn to trust their spiritual eyes more than their physical sight.

The Artist is always at work...even in the midst of a storm.

Can you trust Him?

Going Deeper

(To be answered individually or with a small group.)

• Identify a storm you have experienced in life.
• When were you able to see Jesus working through the storm?
• Was your storm caused by disobedience? Or were you obeying Christ when the storm occurred?
• The disciples learned five lessons from their two storms. Describe what you learned from your personal storm.
• How has the storm strengthened your faith?

Prayer time: Dear Jesus: I want to trust You completely. Even when I can't feel Your presence, I want to know You're with me. And when I can't see You working, help me have faith that You are active. In the midst of my next storm, help me not to ask why. But help me instead ask, "What can I learn from this?" Please increase my faith in You.

CHAPTER
FIFTEEN

Sometimes God acts immediately; other times He waits.

We don't understand His thinking or His timetable.

But the mark of a mature Christian is to accept His ways without understanding.

Time.

It's taken for granted—until it's *you* around whom the hands of the clock revolve.

12 YEARS

(Matthew 9:18-23; Mark 5:21-43)

12 years

4,383 days

6,311,520 minutes

378,691,200 seconds

It's all a matter of perspective.

Twelve years in the life of a child is too short. However, 12 years of dealing with an infirmity is another story. 4,383 days spent watching your daughter grow is brief. 4,383 days of doctor and hospital visits would seem like an eternity. 6,311,520 minutes filled with hope of a future is exciting. 6,311,520 minutes of shattered dreams is excruciating. 378,691,200 seconds in celebration of new experiences is delightful. 378,691,200 seconds in the context of suffering is torture.

Twelve years can pass in the blink of an eye.

Twelve years can last for an eternity.

It's simply a matter of perspective.

As the boat neared the shore, the crowds began to gather. It's quite a different scene from their landing on the other side — the Gentile side of the lake. There they were met by a wild, tormented man that none could tame.

Jesus did.

Here they are met by the crowds overcome by curiosity — a curiosity only Jesus could satisfy. On the other side, the crowds ran Him off. Here they welcome Him with open arms.

Needed: A Miracle

Numbered in the welcoming committee was a man of great importance: Jarius. He was a ruler of the synagogue, a leader of the religious community in that area. As he cut his way through the crowd to the place where Jesus was standing, people were anxious to witness what was about to occur. His urgency and determination were undeniable. Would there be fireworks? A confrontation? What was on his mind? What would this encounter accomplish? What was it about this time?

All questions are addressed as they begin to notice the serious expression on Jarius' face. A hush sweeps across the crowd as they watch this man of standing, now on his knees at Jesus' feet. They hear his trembling voice as he begins to plead:

"My little daughter lies at the point of death. Come and lay Your hands on her, that she may be healed, and she will live"
(Mark 5:23NKJV).

Matthew says it like this:

"My daughter has just died. But come and put your hand on her, and she will live"
(Matthew 9:18 NIV).

By looking at both Matthew and Mark's telling of this story we can more clearly see the source of the urgency, the reason for his haste. What a terrible thing for any parent to have to deal with! Can you feel the heaviness in his heart? Can't you sense the emotion in his words?

"My daughter has just died."

Now we understand why he was walking at an accelerated pace. This was a terribly serious matter at hand…rather, at heart. He has a daughter. We don't learn of her age here, but Mark 5:42 tells us she was merely 12 years of age. Just as the man rushed from the tombs to Jesus' feet, now Jarius does the same. He's begging. He's pleading.

Jesus is moved.

> *"Jesus got up and went with him, and so did his disciples"*
> *(Matthew 9:19 NIV).*

Hope Is Born

Jesus doesn't hesitate to go with Jarius. Excitement moves to another level as the crowd anticipates what's about to happen. In mob-like fashion, they make their way from the lake. Moving together, it's a procession of anticipation, excitement, expectation. Something incredible is about to happen. But it's not what they were expecting.

Across town, there's another story beginning to unfold. Well, it's actually been going on for quite some time. Twelve years to be exact. She can point back to the day it all started.

Something incredible is about to happen. But it's not what they were expecting.

That was the day her life, as she had known, ended. Before that day she was filled with dreams. But now those dreams are a memory. So much time has passed even that memory has faded. Now there was only one way to describe her life: Broken.

She Was Broken Physically

> *"And suddenly, a woman who had a flow of blood for twelve years, came from behind..."*
> *(Matthew 9:20 NKJV).*

Mark adds this:

> *"…and had suffered many things from many physicians"*
> *(Mark 5:25-26 NKJV).*

12 years

4,383 days

6,311,520 minutes

378,691,200 seconds she dealt with this issue.

It wasn't normal. It wasn't right. She tried everything she knew to do. Doctors visited. Prayer after prayer had been prayed. Medicines taken and applied. Home remedies: Two chicken feathers dipped in lamp oil and matted with freshly shorn wool. She tried it all, but nothing would bring the relief she needed and longed for. What hopes were lingering now are beginning to diminish.

She's had her last doctor visit. She was no longer welcome to any physician.

She's had her last doctor visit. She was no longer welcome to any physician.

She Was Broken Financially

> *"She had spent all that she had and was no better, but rather grew worse"*
> *(Mark 5:26 NKJV).*

What little glimmer of hope she may have had in the medical profession was now gone. Considering that even if there were a wonder doctor that relocated to her area, she wouldn't be able to see him. Or if some miracle cure was discovered, some newly researched medical breakthrough, it would be of no help to her. Why? She couldn't afford it. She had written her last check. The bank had closed her account. Everything was gone. She had exhausted her funds. What a mess.

She Was Broken Spiritually

Broken. That's what she was. There's just no other way to put it. Completely broken.

Deserved. That's what they thought. It's a working out of the sin in her life. She must be some sort of pervert receiving God's punishment. He had removed His hand from her life. She saw it in their eyes. The judgment. The disdain. All this had her an emotional wreck.

She Was Broken Relationally

She'd never have a family of her own. Her condition made it impossible. Whatever bed she sat on, she defiled. She was unlovable, unwanted. Certainly she was being punished. She might as well just wait for it all to come to an end.

Broken.

That's what she was. There's just no other way to put it.

Completely broken.

What do you do with broken things?

Throw them out.

Get rid of them.

Carry out the trash.

The garbage must be discarded.

But, not the Artist. He's at work and He sees a masterpiece.

She matters to the Father. He's willing to move heaven and earth to help her. It's all about her.

From Billy:

I met Jody when I was in the tenth grade. I started to attend the youth group he was a part of and we quickly became friends. Great friends actually. The kind of friends that would spend every weekend together. I guess you could say we were some of the best of friends.

Today, Jody is a pastor of a United Methodist Church in Northeast Ohio. For the past few years Jody has invited me to his church for a weekend of renewal. It's a wonderful time. I really enjoy visiting with Jody and his family, just catching up on life. It's hard to believe how time flies. It seems like yesterday we were sitting together in French class or hanging out in my bedroom on a Friday night.

One of my favorite parts of the weekend is the Saturday morning Bible study time we do at the church. It's very casual. We come and gather in the fellowship hall, drink coffee, eat donuts, and talk about God's Word. Some of the most meaningful times in my ministry have occurred during these meetings.

During our last time together, we had a time when people would share a passage of Scripture that has really been meaningful in their lives. It was beautiful to hear the way God's Word had been revealed to be true in lives. One really grabbed my attention. It was Jody's. Here's what he said:

"There are certain verses of the Bible I have remembered over the years due to the impact of God's living Word whispered at just the right moment, just when I needed to hear it. One verse has been particularly impactful because of its daily application in my life throughout childhood. This verse is found in the book of Isaiah, and it was a comfort to a people who were in exile from their home. I, too, have found comfort in my most difficult journeys.

"'But they that wait upon the Lord shall renew their strength; they shall mount up with wings as eagles; they shall run, and not be weary; and they shall walk, and not faint' (Isaiah 40:31 KJV).

"I didn't become a Christian until I was 16 years old. Because my mother hoped in Christ, she took me to Sunday school when she could. Other than a visit to her church now and then, my faith was limited to an unused old Bible that collected dust on my nightstand, along with its bookmark. The Bible was rarely opened, but that bookmark stuck out far beyond the edges and beckoned me to look at it. I often pulled it out and read the print, 'But they that wait upon the Lord…'

"Why was I so attracted to these words found in the middle of a book I never read? The only explanation is that God knew what I needed to hear in the midst of my youth: If I'd wait on Him, someday, somehow, my strength would come. I'd soar like an eagle in this life.

"Those words spoke volumes into my childhood. I needed to know that someday I'd make it. I was in a home with an alcoholic, verbally abusive father. We struggled to make ends meet, and much of the family income was spent on cheap liquor. I wanted freedom from this life—freedom from the abuse. I wanted to soar away—like an eagle.

"Each night that I hid in my room from the fighting, from the seemingly hopeless dark nights, I'd grab my bookmark. I prayed to a God I had yet to trust. I begged, 'If you are real, God, renew my strength!' And the most beautiful thing about my favorite verse is that in a childlike faith to wait on God, He renewed my strength *in the midst of* my hopeless surroundings.

"I didn't need a sober dad, financial security, or a new locale. God met me right there, while I held tightly to that old bookmark. My life soared in renewal, just as He promised."

12 years
4,383 days
6,311,520 minutes
378,691,200 seconds

That's how long she'd been waiting, how long she'd suffered. That's how long she'd been broken. But today something's about to change.

"When she heard about Jesus, she came behind Him in the crowd
and touched His garment. For she said,
'If only I may touch His clothes, I shall be made well'"
(Mark 5:27-28).

With the words "If only..." on her tongue, she makes her way to Jesus. I'm sure her heart sinks as she sees the crowd crushing in. She uses what little strength she has to edge her way through that crowd. They're relentless. She's weak, frail.

Tossed around like a ping-pong ball, she pushes her way through. In an instant she's thrown to her knees, but she can't stop. She's almost there. When she gets within arm's length of Jesus, she reaches out her trembling hand and grabs the edge of His garment.

"Immediately the fountain of her blood was dried up,
and she felt in her body that she was healed of the affliction"
(Mark 5:29).

Immediately.

In an instant what she had given everything for, she received. What she had sought after for 12 long years she found in a touch of the Artist. Reworked. Restored. She came to Him in pieces, now she leaves in His peace.

An unexpected interruption.

That's the only way you can describe what just happened.

Back to the Beginning

Don't forget how this story began: Jarius came to Jesus begging Him to move in his daughter's life—a life that had only been lived twelve years. Jarius and Jesus were on the move.

Then this: An unexpected interruption.

How much time had passed? How long did Jarius stand waiting for the scene to play out? From his point of view, precious time was being stolen for an opportunity for his little girl to be made well. Life has been too short; there were still firsts to be experienced, discoveries to be made, dreams to be fulfilled, hopes to be realized. Now this woman had robbed them from time. Time they didn't have. All his worst fears were soon realized.

"While He was still speaking, some came from the ruler of the synagogue's
house who said, 'Your daughter is dead. Why trouble the Teacher any
further?'"
(Mark 5:35 NKJV)

Dead.

It's too late now.

12 short years of life.

4,383 days of discovery.

6,311,520 minutes developing into a young lady.

378,691,200 seconds dreaming of what the future would hold.

It's gone now.

She's gone.

The time for healing has past.   ***The Artist is at work.***

How could this happen? Everything

was going to be okay. Jesus was coming

to touch his little girl. But then *she* came.

Interrupted. She stole his daughters healing. I can't help but wonder

what Jarius was thinking, feeling. Overwhelmed with sorrow.

Consumed with anger. Confused. Now what?

Remember, it's all a matter of perspective.

The Artist is at work.

> *"As soon as Jesus heard the word that was spoken, He said to*
> *the ruler of the synagogue, 'Do not be afraid; only believe'"*
> *(Mark 5:36 NKJV).*

Only believe.

It's easy to get hung up on those words. How could he believe? They've come and said it was too late, she's dead. Not sick, not close to death, but dead. His worst fears have been realized. His urgency was for nothing. Because of an interruption all hope was gone. Believe?

Let's stop here for a moment.

Believe?

She's dead. Not dying. Not sick.

She's...dead.

Sometimes believing can be the hardest thing we have to do.

The doctor says there's no way.

Believe.

The bills are due and the money is gone.

Believe.

Everything is going to work out even though it's spinning out of control.

Believe.

You are a Masterpiece even when everything seems broken and out of place.

Believe.

Sometimes believing is the hardest thing to do.

From Billy:

Sometimes it's really hard to trust. Not because you don't *want* to, but because it's hard. When I took the step of leaving my youth pastor position to enter the field of fulltime evangelism, I knew it would be quite a leap. I'd be leaving the stability of a set income, benefits and staff, to enter into a new world of uncertainty. But I believed it was where God was leading me.

People weren't so encouraging: "You'll starve to death!"

"No one knows who you are!"

"You'd better think this through!"

And these were my friends! They were concerned. They were being honest. But I knew what God wanted me to do so I did it.

The first year was pretty interesting. I remember two

weeks I spent in the upper peninsula of Michigan: Two weeks, three churches, three revivals. When I received my pay for those two weeks, it didn't even cover my expenses. I couldn't help but wonder if my friends were right. *Would* I starve to death? Frustrated, I began the journey from Escanaba, Mich., back home to Cincinnati.

That was a long Sunday night. Discouragement seemed to scream inside my brain every mile I drove. The voices of the *encouragers* grew stronger as the minutes passed. To top it off, as I pulled into the Cincinnati city limits Monday around 9 a.m., my car began to sputter. I was scheduled to be in Arkansas in a day, so I definitely needed my car working properly.

I called the dealership and went over my finances. All I had to spare was $100. It would be impossible to fix! It would cost me $100 just that to have the problem diagnosed. But it had to be done.

I dropped it off at the dealership,

walked across the street to a shopping center,

and I waited for the call.

It was finally ready. I started across the parking lot. It was a sunny day, and as I walked, I noticed something sparkling on the ground. It was a quarter. I picked it up. A few steps later I saw something else: a penny. I picked it up. By the time I reached the dealership I had found a quarter and four pennies: $.29.

I approached the attendant and he said, "Mr. Huddleston, the charge for the servicing of your vehicle today is $100.29."

Sometimes it's hard to trust, but God is *always* trustworthy.

Only believe.

That's what Jesus said.

That's what Jarius does.

They continue to the home where a little girl's life has seemingly come to an end. When they approach, the mourning process has begun. In fact, it was in full swing:

> *"Then He came to the house of the ruler of the synagogue,*
> *and saw a tumult and those who wept and wailed loudly"*
> *(Mark 5:38 NKJV).*

The scene was loud and confusing.

Disorder was running rampant.

Weeping and wailing. Why? Her life was no more.

Still, Jesus said, "Believe."

This is a scene you could easily get lost in. The hysteria and sorrow had taken up residency in this home. Grief had began to cast its shadow in every corner of this house. Vibrant, bright colors have been replaced by shades of grey. But now the Artist is here.

He walks to where the little girl is lying.

He reaches out and grips her cold hand.

The Artist speaks:

> *"Little girl, I say to you, arise"*
> *(Mark 5:41 NKJV).*

Life courses from Jesus to the little girl. A heart that had ceased to function begins to beat again. Blood that had halted its flow begins to race throughout living veins. Flesh that had grown cold from death is now flourishing with the warmth of new life.

It's hard to believe, but…

She's alive!

The masterpiece is restored!

What an incredible day.

Two stories of:

12 years

4,383 days

6,311,520 minutes

378,691,200 seconds

One story was much too short. The other lasted for an eternity.

Both mattered to the Artist.

It was simply a matter of perspective.

Going Deeper

(To be answered individually or with a small group.)

- Describe a specific time you experienced a need of desperation (like Billy and his car). How long did you have to live in that circumstance?
- Share about a time in your life when all you could do was trust.
- Do you remember some of the feelings that accompanied that need? Were you lonely? Anxious? Scared?
- When did you find an answer and how did you find it?
- What did your circumstance teach you about trust? Determination?

Prayer time: Jesus, thank You for caring about every area of my life. Thank You that I'll never have a need that's impossible for You. Help me to be more determined in bringing *all* my needs to You on a daily basis. Please bring me to a place of trust in every area of my relationship with you. I really long to be a follower who's able to believe even when it may seem unbelievable. Thank You again for caring about me.

CHAPTER
SIXTEEN

Jesus crossed a lake simply to restore wholeness to an outcast.

When you find yourself making your home in a graveyard, your self-esteem is at an all-time low.

His identity was among the dead.

Even today it's easy to become so accustomed to living in the darkness we fail to realize where we are.

And sometimes we get so comfortable wearing shackles, we begin to accessorize them.

GET OUTTA THE GRAVEYARD!

(Luke 8:26-39; Mark 5:1-20)

Most of us go to the cemetery for one reason—to mourn the dead. So we're completely caught off guard by the silhouette of a man hovering in the hazy morning light. He has actually made his home among the tombstones. We can imagine his day began just like his day

He has actually made his home among the tombstones.

before: After scavenging for anything to eat—berries, possibly a piece of unripened fruit—or maybe he even roasted part of a dead rodent for breakfast, he moved in and out of the morning shadows and between graves.

His life is meaningless.

He. Has. No. Hope.

He's exactly where the Master's enemy wants him:

in total desperation.

He's living in a graveyard.

But though today has begun like any other, it will end completely different. Today is the day his life will be forever different. Forever changed. Forever whole.

Today is the day He'll meet the Master Artist.

Color will once again fill his life.

His smeared existence on the canvas will be restored with vivacity.

His eyes are usually downcast, focused on the ground. But for a second he looks up. And in that second, he sees the One who will give him his life back.

We'll use both versions of his story—from Mark and from Luke—to take a closer look at his life.

"They sailed to the region of the Gerasenes, which is across the lake from Galilee. When Jesus stepped ashore, he was met by a demon-possessed man from the town"
(Luke 8:26-27 NIV).

He approached Jesus.

This tormented, vile, despicable outcast approached the Son of God.

Don't ever think you can't approach Jesus. You serve a Savior who is extremely relational. Next to His Father God, Jesus loves people more than anything.

The Artist welcomes you. And His brush is always wet with new paint for the cracks that appear on your canvas. He's into total restoration. What He creates is beauty; you are no exception.

Jesus is always approachable. And *anyone* can approach Him.

Jesus hadn't even climbed out of the boat before He was met by this tormented man whom society had dubbed a freak. Perhaps Andrew had tossed the anchor over the side of the boat. Maybe James and John were putting on their tunics after feeling the sun on their backs. We can imagine Jesus lifting His robe and raising His leg to climb over the side. But *as He's climbing—before He's even out of the boat*—the outcast is before Him.

> *Jesus is always approachable. And anyone can approach Him.*

He obviously didn't get many visitors in the cemetery. And the question we're begging to ask is, "Why is Jesus even *at* the graveyard?" He wasn't burying anyone. There's no indication of a funeral. There are no shops. No business being conducted. No synagogues to visit.

Could it be the only reason He showed up in the graveyard was to restore this despicable, broken man?

That's not hard to believe. It's what He does. He goes to great lengths to bring wholeness to His creation. Look at what *God* did! He moved heaven and earth—by sacrificing His only Son—just to save *you*. Going out of His way is as natural as breathing. Making special trips is at the top of His itinerary.

He's in pursuit of you. You matter to Him.

He's determined to offer you wholeness.

He'll travel across a lake or across a world to find you.

It's the Master Artist in motion.

Without hesitation.

A Disturbance Deep Within

The madman is possessed by demons. Personified evil breathes and moves inside him. As he approaches Jesus, the supernatural force senses holiness is near.

Evil reacts.

Something's wrong.

The demons are thrashing and trouncing rebelliously inside the man. His flesh tingles. His hair stands on end. His body is consumed with violent chills. There's a turbulent disturbance in the supernatural demonic force within—all become Jesus is near.

He's in pursuit of you. You matter to Him.

You see, the last person a demon wants to see is Jesus Christ, the Son of God. The enemy despises the Master's approach, knowing He will bring restoration to the ruined and ostracized man.

But sure enough…

pulling right up to the shore…

in a boat...

climbing over the side...

is Jesus Christ, the Master Artist Himself.

"This man lived among the gravestones and had such strength that whenever he was put into handcuffs and shackles—as he often was—he snapped the handcuffs from his wrists and smashed the shackles and walked away. No one was strong enough to control him"
(Mark 5:3-4 TLB).

Because of the supernatural evil power within him, whenever he was bound with ropes, he snapped them like dental floss. So people had shackled him, but he still broke free.

Nothing New

"All day long and through the night he would wander among the tombs and in the wild hills, screaming and cutting himself with sharp pieces of stones"
(Mark 5:5 TLB).

Did you know that cutting is nothing new? The first cutters are mentioned in the Bible. This outcast was a cutter. But he's not the only biblical character to cut. Flash back to 1 Kings 18. We're inside Mount Carmel Arena. It's a showdown between the godly prophet Elijah and the evil prophets of the idol Baal.

The rules: Both teams have a dead bull on stage.

Neither team can use fire-starting resources.

Both teams will pray.

The sovereignty who burns the bull is the one true God.

The prophets of Baal aren't having any luck. Elijah is impatient.

He begins to taunt them. Let's look at their reaction:

"So they shouted louder and, as was their custom, cut themselves with knives and swords until the blood gushed out. They raved all afternoon until the time of the evening sacrifice, but there was no reply, no voice, no answer"
(1 Kings 18:28-29 TLB).

He was experiencing extreme loneliness and massive aloneness. Two different things. Both devastating.

The prophets of Baal were cutters. Satan's goal is ALWAYS destruction. He not only wants to destroy the inside of a person; He wants to destroy the outside as well. The man in the graveyard was a cutter. Satan was destroying him inside and out.

Cutting isn't new. It's never the answer. But Jesus understands the pain and turmoil that brings a person to cut. He understands this kind of deep, intense, emotional agony. And He yearns to heal.

What Else?

This ostracized outcast is not only living with evil as his driving force, but he's also destroying his physical body. In addition to that, he's homeless and naked. Completely destitute.

He has nothing.

He is living in a cemetery!

What does this say about him? Obviously, he has no hope. And obviously he's in a major identity crisis. To make one's home in a graveyard is saying, "I'm dead. This is where I belong. This is my identity."

He was experiencing extreme loneliness and massive aloneness.

SUSIE SHELLENBERGER | BILLY HUDDLESTON

Two different things. Both devastating.

He's apart from friends, family and society. His culture wants nothing to do with him. He's not even accepted among the outcasts! He's a freak. He has been chained by society—that's their answer. He's in a horrible condition. And the Enemy is in complete charge of his life. The Destroyer is slowly destroying the inside and outside of this man's existence.

Way Back When

We're not told how he became like this, but don't you wonder? If we could trace his timeline, we might see he was abused as a child. Or we may discover he was traumatized by divorce. Perhaps he was bullied incessantly. Maybe someone close to him died. Did he become so angry—or so hurt—that he gave Satan a foothold?

If we don't surrender our pain to Jesus, it eventually destroys us. And the longer we hold onto it, the greater the opportunity Satan has to control more of our existence.

"Then Jesus spoke to the demon within the man and said, 'Come out, you evil spirit.' It gave a terrible scream, shrieking, 'What are you going to do to me, Jesus, Son of the Most High God? For God's sake, don't torture me!'"
(Mark 5:7-8 TLB)

The demons are controlling the man's tongue and voice, and they're speaking directly to Jesus.

"Jesus asked him, 'What is your name?'
'Legion,' he replied, because many demons had gone into him"
(Luke 8:30 NIV).

Jesus knows everything. He knew what the man was called. But He still asked the question, because Jesus cherishes dialogue. You serve a relational Savior. He can't wait to hear you pray. He yearns for conversation with His creation. He places top value on interaction with you.

Legion.

That's a weird name for someone.

In those days, a legion equaled six thousand soldiers. There may have actually been six thousand demons inside this man...or it could simply be the demons' way of saying there were so many even they had lost count. The name Legion indicates how serious his condition was. It's proof Satan had complete control of the outcast and even robbed him of a name and slapped a label on him instead.

Jesus cherishes dialogue.

Satan had stolen his identity. He had been reduced to nothing more than a label. Unfortunately, you may know what it's like to be known by a label:

—the divorced one

—the girl who had an abortion

—the overweight person

—the out-of-work dad

—the alcoholic

—the one with the eating disorder

—the addict

Jesus never calls you by a label! Isaiah 43, 44 and 45 tell us He calls you by your *name*. He reminds you that you've been chosen by Him, that you're special, and that He speaks your name! Refuse to allow Satan to replace your identity with a label. Perhaps you used to live defined by a label. But 2 Corinthians 5:17 tells us when we come to

Christ, we become a brand-new creation. We are no longer defined by our lifestyle, our failures, or our sin. We are defined by the Son of God.

Conflict

The next few verses show the demons begging Jesus to go away and not to send them to the bottomless pit. So the man's words say one thing (his voice being controlled by Satan), and his actions say the opposite.

His actions—falling at the feet of Jesus—say, "I need You! Something's not right. Please help me!" But his words are screaming the opposite: "Go away! Leave me alone."

There's obviously an extreme spiritual battle going on. Maybe you can identify. Have there been times when you've felt God's nudging to move forward, yet the carnal nature wants to hold you back? Spiritual warfare is constant. Satan doesn't care about those who aren't Christians. The ones he's after are the believers, the Christ-followers. When you experience similar conflict, yield to the Holy Spirit's direction. He's bringing you closer to the Master for restoration.

We are no longer defined by our lifestyle, our failures, or our sin. We are defined by the Son of God.

The demons were afraid, because they knew who Jesus was. They knew that whenever Jesus shows up, things change! Jesus Himself said that He came to stir things up (see Luke 12:51).

So the demons try to strike a deal with Jesus. They don't want to be destroyed. They try to convince Jesus into casting them inside a herd of nearby pigs. Jesus did that.

The result?

The pigs ran squealing down a large slope into the lake and drowned.

Jesus doesn't make deals.

With anyone.

Restoration

Let's fast-forward:

"When they came to Jesus, they found the man from whom the demons had gone out, sitting at Jesus' feet, dressed and in his right mind; and they were afraid"

(Luke 8:35 NIV).

There's often a godly fear and wonder when Jesus works. We're not accustomed to seeing the supernatural happen and when it does, we sometimes react in fear. No one had been able to help this man. We can only guess how many years he spent tagged as "the freak in the graveyard."

But at the name of JESUS, the demons had to flee.

Restoration began:

Insanity gone and clarity bestowed.

Nakedness clothed with garments of forgiveness.

Madness replaced with peace.

Sanity. Wholeness. Freedom.

No more shackles. No more shame.

The Artist repairing His painting.

The Father proving your value.

Jesus got in the boat to leave. The man wanted to go with Him, but Jesus refused.

"Jesus sent him away, saying, 'Return home and tell how much God has done for you.' So the man went away and told all over town how much Jesus had done for him"

(Luke 8:38-39 NIV).

It's much easier to say, "I'm going to Mexico to serve Jesus and tell people what He has done for me," than it is to say, "I'm going to carry my Bible to work tomorrow and share with my colleagues the difference He has made in my life."

Mexico is exciting. Beautiful beaches. Full of adventure.

Your neighborhood, your work place, not so much. But Jesus wants to see His masterpiece thriving in the midst of home. That's the beginning. That's the test. That's where the rubber meets the road.

In essence, Jesus was instructing the man to *leave the graveyard.*

Guess what—He says the same thing to you!

Get outta the graveyard.

Jesus didn't create you for death; He created you for life.

His plan is not among the dead; it's in the midst of the living.

The problem?

Many of us have become so comfortable where we are, we've failed to see our location. We've become so accustomed to living among tombstones of compromise and sin and labels and defeat and fear and addictions that we haven't even noticed we've set up housekeeping right inside the graveyard.

> *Jesus didn't create you for death; He created you for life.*

We've become so used to our shackles that we've started to accessorize them.

We've become so used to our shackles that we've started to accessorize them.

We've become so used to our shackles that we've started to accessorize them.

Yes, that triple repeat was intentional. We've talked ourselves into believing the shackles are simply a part of our wardrobe. We've convinced ourselves we actually need this stronghold in our lives.

We weren't meant to live in shackles. We are meant to live in victory! You were created for freedom.

So
get
out
of
the
graveyard.

What Will it Take?

Wouldn't you love to know the man's actual name? Did he go from Legion to Larry? Was it Eric, Bruce, Josh, Ryan, or Grant? The new name isn't important; his actions are the issue. Verse 20 tells us he obeyed the Master; he left the graveyard and told everyone what Jesus had done for him.

You're probably not dealing with thousands of demons. But it could be you've accepted a label for yourself instead of being the beautiful and whole person God created. Maybe you're struggling with your identity—you see yourself as blurred, discontent, less than. Perhaps you can relate to being shackled—emotionally, relationally, or vocationally. Or maybe you feel as though you're living in a graveyard—a place that's far less than God's ideal for you.

What will it take for you to leave your shackles behind?

Go ahead.

Walk away from the tombstones that have been your identity.

Get outta the graveyard.

Going Deeper

(To be answered individually or with a small group.)

- How does it make you feel to know you can approach Jesus anytime, anywhere, about anything?
- Describe the most recent time you approached Him with a specific issue.
- Identify a time when you too, faced a spiritual battle of opposites (you felt His nudge to go forward, but you felt conflicted to remain motionless or to go the opposite direction). This is spiritual warfare.
- Describe a painful event in your life you've struggled giving completely to God. Has Satan tried to gain a foothold in your life because of this struggle?
- What labels have you succumbed to?
- What things tend to shackle you or keep you from becoming all God wants you to be?
- How are you sharing what Jesus has done for you in your home, your workplace, your neighborhood?
- What will it take for you to get out of the graveyard? Are you willing to leave?
- Jesus crossed an entire lake to get to Legion. He'll cross a lake, an ocean, a continent, or a planet to meet your needs. It's all about you. What's your response to this?

Prayer time: Ask God to reveal the identity of your shackles to you. Tell Him of your desire to live in freedom and victory. Seek His forgiveness for becoming comfortable with things in your life that have kept you from intimacy with Him. Ask Him to remove your shackles and lead you out of the graveyard

CHAPTER
SEVENTEEN

You know your strengths, and you're using them well. But even strong Christians face temptation. Disciples are not exempt from fear and confusion. Oftentimes we're simply not as strong as we think we are. When you're at the end of your rope, trust the One who's holding it.

DEVASTATED BUT NOT DESTROYED
(Luke 22:54-62)

"Having arrested Jesus, they led Him and brought Him into the high priest's house. But Peter followed at a distance. Now when they had kindled a fire in the midst of the courtyard and sat down together, Peter sat among them. And a certain servant girl, seeing him as he sat by the fire, looked intently at him and said, "This man was also with Him."

But he denied Him, saying, "Woman, I do not know Him."

And after a little while another saw him and said, "You also are of them." But Peter said, "Man, I am not!"

Then after about an hour had passed, another confidently affirmed, saying, "Surely this fellow also was with Him, for he is a Galilean."

But Peter said, "Man, I do not know what you are saying!" Immediately, while he was still speaking, the rooster crowed. And the Lord turned and looked at Peter. Then Peter remembered the word of the Lord, how He had said to him, "Before the rooster crows, you will deny Me three times." So Peter went out and wept bitterly"

(Luke 22:54-62 NKJV).

All four Gospels are filled with stories about Peter. In fact you'll find that besides Jesus, no one is mentioned as often. That's pretty impressive, huh? There's more. Can you guess whom we have a record of Jesus speaking to more than any other disciple? You've got it: Peter.

Sometimes the words Jesus spoke were words of praise unlike He had spoken to any other. Yet at other times they were words of confrontation and correction. He spoke harder words to Peter than He spoke to any other of the disciples. And yet, this is the man whom Jesus Himself named the Rock and gave great promise. Peter was the stone chosen by the Builder, the Artist Himself.

Think About It

Twelve disciples.

Yet only Simon was renamed by Jesus.

It was during their first recorded encounter this name change occurred. Andrew brings his brother to Jesus telling Him Jesus was the One they'd been waiting for.

> "...when Jesus looked at him, He said, "You are Simon the son of Jonah. You shall be called Cephas' (which is translated, A Stone)"
> (John 1:42).

Right there, on the spot, Jesus gives Simon and new name. Incredible. Why? Because when we hear Jesus speak, He first reveals the reality of who Simon was—the son of Jonah. That was obvious. It was how he was known.

But then Jesus goes on, "You shall be called Cephas." He was unveiling who he was to become. It's pretty incredible to realize that the Artist sees us where we are, who we are, but refuses to leave us there. He sees the potential of what He dreams us to become as only the Artist can.

Flash Back

We see the same thing in the Old Testament story of Gideon. He's hiding in a winepress—afraid of the Midianites. Yet when God speaks to Gideon through an angel, notice how He addresses him:

> "'The Lord is with you, mighty warrior'"
> (Judges 6:12 NIV).

Ha! Gideon is anything, BUT a mighty warrior! He was the least in his family and society saw him as a loser. Yet God called him by what He created him to be.

Though others may only see a blob of paint on a canvas, the Artist knows the beauty of what He is creating you to be and He always calls you by the finished product.

Others see you as a piece of unfinished work. The Artist knows what you're becoming, because He's still painting you. He's not finished with you yet.

Michelangelo was an Italian sculptor, painter, artist, and poet during the Renaissance. He was the epitome of a true renaissance man. He's considered to be one of the greatest artists of all time. Two of his best-known works are sculptures he completed before he even reached the age of thirty: the Pietà and David. In these two works you can sense the merging of what's been said to be two of his great passions: The material beauty of stone or marble, and his belief in God, the Holy and everlasting.

Michelangelo longed to preserve the integrity of the stone block believing that this was where a great sculpture is developed: from within the stone. Nothing would need to be added to it; the beauty, the masterpiece would be found within. It would just take the vision of the artist, the chipping away, until the masterpiece is completed, and the artist's dream realized.

Where others see the exterior, the Artist sees the potential.

What's In a Name?

The Gospels paint an extremely vivid picture of Peter. There are times where we see him as Simon, his name before his encounter with Jesus. It's during these times that we view how very human he is. It's almost as though, in those moments, we see raw human nature shining through and controlling his life.

Then there are those times we see him as Simon Peter. In these times we catch a glimpse of the struggle—the battle between the old and the new. Who we are, *the old man*, struggling with who we are meant to be. It's referred to in many different ways, this battle between human nature and godly control. Or the battle between the flesh and spirit.

It's a struggle we all face.

And it's in this place many of us often relate to Simon Peter.

Ultimately, we see him as Peter—the man whom Jesus longs for him to be. Here we're able to catch glimpses of the Artist's dream being realized. We see the rock in which the gates of hell shall not prevail! During those times he seems unshakeable. It's an image of the Spirit-controlled man. We see the Master Artist performing His incredible transforming work from within, chipping away at the stone, until the masterpiece is complete.

And Then There's Simon Peter

When you begin to examine the story of Simon, there's no question he was an honest, hard-working man. When we first meet him, we discover he's a fisherman.

We often talk about fishermen in these New Testament times as being the uneducated, simple type. But Peter was no slouch. He'd spend his days in the elements casting and drawing the net. He worked by the strength of his back, the sweat of his brow. He'd put in an honest day's labor to earn an honest day's pay. It was physical, tiring work. It was his business. Literally.

Simon was part of the family fishing business. Along with his brother, Andrew, they owned the boats and nets. They had business sense. Remember, it was his partner and brother, Andrew that came to him to introduce him to Jesus.

Under the direction of John the Baptist, Andrew went after Jesus and didn't want his brother to miss out. All through the story it seems as though Simon feels at home on the water, casting and drawing the net; fishing. It's what seemed to define him at times. A fisherman, hardworking and honest. But there is much more to this man.

What Else?

If there's anything that can be said to be true about Simon, it's that he was a passionate man. Throughout the stories we encounter the intensity of his personality. Just as he dominated the fishing expeditions, he dominates the gospels. He's always the first to act, the first to speak. He's comfortable in the spotlight.

He's extreme.

He's an extrovert.

He's impulsive.

He's spontaneous.

And from the foot-washing scene, to his confrontation with Malchus in the garden, you sense the deeply held beliefs and witness Simon's strong emotions.

Jesus the Messiah

One of the occasions where Simon's passion is most evident is in his confession of Jesus as the Christ. Do you remember the story? It's found in Matthew 16.

Jesus has been about Kingdom business. He'd been dealing with the crowds, teaching, touching, changing lives. The excitement was building. Remember, the Jewish people were looking for a Deliverer and they thought Jesus just might be the One. Of course, they were looking for a political figure, someone to free them from the tyranny of

Caesar.

Jesus came to deliver. That's not up for debate. But He came not to deliver in a political manner. Rather, He came to deliver people from true tyranny: The tyranny of sin and self.

From Susie:

I'll never forget when I accepted Christ's forgiveness for my sins. I was in fourth grade.

And I'll never forget when I understood the meaning of it. I was a freshman in high school.

I was privileged to be brought up in a two-parent Christian home. My brother and I loved going to church. We had an amazing children's ministry and an active, large youth ministry.

One Sunday evening, our junior choir sang in the worship service. After singing, we usually left the choir loft and returned to the congregational seating to be with our parents. But for some reason, we were left in the choir loft for the remainder of the service. I didn't pay much attention to the sermon, but I guess Lynette did. She was sitting next to me, and she was a fifth-grader.

At the end of the service, our pastor gave an invitation to all who wanted to be forgiven of their sins. Lynette turned to me and said, "Susie, will you walk down to the altar with me?"

What?! That's the last thing I wanted to do. It was a long walk, and we'd be walking in front of the whole church (about a thousand people). But I was afraid to say no to a fifth-grader, so I made the walk.

My parents saw me go forward and my dad came to pray with me. He knelt beside me and guided me in a prayer of asking Christ to forgive my sins and reign in my heart.

As a fourth-grader, I wasn't totally sure about all that happened. I was simply happy I was headed for heaven someday. Let's fast-forward to my freshman year in high school.

We had a female speaker for our Sunday evening service. Besides a missionary, I'd never heard a female speaker before. Her name was Ann Kiemel. She was mesmerizing. She spoke so simply, yet the message to follow Christ was so compelling.

At the end of the service, she asked us to forget about who was sitting next to us and to simply stand and say aloud, "Yes, Lord" if we were serious about following Christ.

I stood.

"Yes, Lord."

I began carrying my Bible with me to my public school. I invited others to church with me. I got excited about reading God's Word and discovered how thrilling it is to be a Christian. My sins had been paid for. Christ loved me more than I could imagine. I wanted to show Him how grateful I was by loving and obeying Him.

I've never looked back.

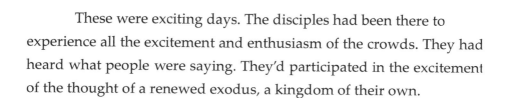

These were exciting days. The disciples had been there to experience all the excitement and enthusiasm of the crowds. They had heard what people were saying. They'd participated in the excitement of the thought of a renewed exodus, a kingdom of their own.

In the midst of it all, Jesus is going to reveal more about Himself to His disciples. Let's listen in on a conversation He and the disciples have:

"[Jesus] asked His disciples, saying, 'Who do men say that I, the Son of Man, am?'

So they said, 'Some say John the Baptist, some Elijah, and others Jeremiah or one of the prophets.'

He said to them, 'But who do you say that I am?'

Simon Peter answered and said, 'You are the Christ, the Son of the living God'"

(Matthew 16:13-16 NKJV).

He couldn't hold it in. Without even waiting for discussion from the others, Simon blurts it out.

He's sure.

Decisive.

Determined.

While others are speculating with the crowds, Simon speaks from his heart. But the conversation's not over. Jesus quickly affirms him, yet He lets the disciple know this thought didn't come totally from him. God, the Father, planted it in his heart. And good for Simon! He was listening to the higher voice.

Others were distracted by the voices around them, but Simon was already tuned in to Jehovah God's still small voice. But the conversation still isn't over.

Remember the Scene?

Jesus and the twelve are talking about crowds and kingdoms. For the first time in their walk with Him, Jesus has revealed who He is, and now He develops the plan. He announces they're going to Jerusalem where He will suffer, bleed and ultimately die at the hand of the religious leadership. But Jesus also states He'll be raised on the third day. He's revealed His Person and now He unveils His purpose.

This is a hard pill for Simon to swallow. He takes Jesus aside and speaks to Him. Scripture actually says that he began to rebuke Jesus.

Rebuke Jesus.

Wow.

Let's listen in:

"Far be it from You, Lord; this shall not happen to You!"
(Matthew 16:22 NKJV)

Do you sense his heart? He has just proclaimed Jesus to be the Christ, something he'd been waiting to do. Now he doesn't understand. He doesn't think it should play out this way.

Never.

Not like this.

Listen to how Jesus responds:

"Get behind Me, Satan!"
(Matthew 16:23 NKJV)

There they are.

The harshest words Jesus spoke to any of the disciples. Peter's passion was obvious. He was definitely a passionate man.

Honest and hard working? No question.

Devoted? Certainly so.

Determined? Of course.

Simon Was Committed

Once Simon made the decision to follow after Jesus, it was final. He left *all* to follow Him. He committed in his heart and determined in his mind, He would follow Christ. He placed his trust in his new Master. He was there in the garden on the night of His betrayal. It was he who drew his sword and cut off the ear of Malchus. He was willing to battle for his King…to die.

So many descriptive words can be used.

So many things could be said.

But one stands out: Simon was a devastated man.

Of all the adjectives that can be used, this one stands out. It's the bolded letters on the pages of Simon's story. The exclamation point of his walk.

Without a doubt: devastated.

If we were able to sit down and have a one-on-one with this man and ask him what he regrets most, this would be it. This is the point in his life where he is everything he said he wouldn't be.

Jesus called him the Rock.

Yet Simon knows he's simply shifting sand.

His Story

Let's take a few steps back and remember the story together, okay?

It's the night Jesus is betrayed in the garden. From a distance, Simon follows Jesus and His captors to the court of the High Priest where Jesus would be tried. Out of 12—he's the only one there. He doesn't want to lose sight of his Master.

With one eye on the events playing out and another on the gathering crowd, he settles by a coal fire that had been kindled in the courtyard. This fire will serve as a place of warmth from the cool night air. It will illuminate the darkness and provide light. It will also provide a place of sustenance—a place where those gathered near can warm their bread and cakes. This fire becomes a place of conversation about the events that are unfolding. It's here that the fire becomes a place of confrontation.

Three times Simon is confronted.

First a woman.

Then a man.

And one last time...

The response from Simon was the same:

"I DO NOT KNOW HIM."

Three times confronted.

Three times denied.

Then the rooster crows.

Do you sense the intensity? Remember what Luke said:

"Immediately, while he was still speaking, the rooster crowed. And the Lord turned and looked at Peter. Then Peter remembered the word of the Lord, how He had said to him, 'Before the rooster crows, you will deny Me three times.' So Peter went out and wept bitterly"
(Luke 22:60-62 NKJV).

After the third denial, as the last syllable was thrown from his tongue, Jesus looks at Peter. His eyes sear straight into the disciple's heart.

Memories are stirred: He had done exactly what he said he would not.

A man is broken: He weeps bitter, intense tears.

It all happened at the rooster's crow.

The rooster's crow. A daily reminder of his greatest failure burned into his memory, replayed every time a rooster would crow. He could not escape. It was his new reality.

Failure.

Broken.

Lost.

Devastated.

Unable to escape his feelings he does the only thing he knows to do: He goes back to his old routine. He gets back into the boat. He returns to fishing. His story is a sad one at this point. It seems he'll have to live with the consequences of his actions for the rest of his life. He had his memories of better days, better times. But now, he was here.

Can You Relate?

Don't we all have things in our lives we regret? And no matter how hard we try, we can't seem to escape. A song, a location, an individual, even a specific scent can transport us to the time of our greatest failures.

From Billy:

I was preaching in revival at a church in Southeastern Ohio. It's a great church that over the years I have built a relationship with and been blessed to have many return visits. I'll never forget an encounter I had with a lady during my second visit there.

It was after the Sunday evening service and the church was having a fellowship time following the revival. We gathered in the gymnasium where tables were set up and food was prepared. The line reached into the hallway as people anxiously awaited the opportunity to fill their plates with the food that had been prepared. Having been delayed at my product table I took my place at the end of the line.

I began to chat with the lady standing in front of me. She had an interesting story. She was probably old enough to be my grandmother, so I was intrigued to hear just a little about her life.

She began by telling me how wonderful God has been to her. She shared how she and her husband had the privilege of serving in ministry together for many years. This sweet lady recounted how God had allowed them to reach out to orphans, start schools and orphanages in the name of Jesus. Countless lives were touched. Circumstances were changed. God was blessing, moving. Until it happened. Her husband left her for another woman. I could tell in the sound of her voice the pain she experienced. It was obvious by the look in her eyes the devastation she felt. My heart went out to her.

The cadence of her story began to increase as she began to state she had been praying for her husband now for nearly 26 years. Twenty six years! How wonderful that even through all the pain, the hurt, the betrayal, she still longed for everything to be well between her former husband and God! But then it happened. Her tone of voice changed, "I've been praying for 26 years that he would stand in front of all our family and friends—everyone— and admit what he has done to me!"

This was her rooster's crow. Twenty six years of her life gone, controlled, claimed.

She was unable to let it go. She held on to the devastation.

What's Your Rooster's Crow?

These are stories that could be rehearsed over and over again. Countless lives affected by the choices we've made, or what others have done to us. Questions run through our minds like children at a school playground:

How could God use me when I've...

What would so and so think of me if they knew?

Who am I to do anything after where I've been?

Why would Jesus love me when I'm so...

Every rooster's crow reminds us. We're haunted by the memories of the past. Conditioned to think we'll never be good enough, never able to be who He intends us to be. We go back to the comfort of the old routine.

Just like Peter.

Hang On!

But that's not the end of the story. It wasn't for Simon. It's not for you. The Artist sees beyond the exterior to the masterpiece on the inside.

Peter and some of the guys had spent another long, lonely night out on the sea. Casting the net.

Drawing the net.

Casting the net.

Drawing the net.

Same old routine.

When daybreak came (see John 21), they begin rowing toward shore and notice One standing there waiting. There's a familiar conversation in the boat, and they realize it's Jesus.

Simon Peter is overcome. Unable to wait for the boat to get there, he jumps into the water and swims to Jesus. (He would've walked, but that didn't work out so well last time he was on top of the water.) Jesus has prepared a coal fire. (Remember the scene in the high priests' court?)

This fire would be a place of warmth, for Peter to dry out and the others to chase away the coolness of a night. The last bit of darkness from the long night before would be chased away by its illuminating flames. It would be a place for sustenance—Jesus had prepared breakfast. It would serve as a place for conversation.

Three questions. Do you love me?

Three affirmations. Yes I do.

Jesus is recreating the scene of Simon's greatest failure.

Don't miss this. When did He come?

At daybreak. When the rooster crows.

(Do you have goose bumps?)

What a Savior!

Jesus had reclaimed what the enemy had cornered off! The long, dark night of failure in Peter's life had come to an end. He was devastated, but he was *not* destroyed.

Reinstated and affirmed by the Artist, the shifting sand begins to take on a solid rock foundation. This Rock would go on to write two books of the Bible, spread Christianity, plant early churches, disciple new believers, and duplicate the miracles of His master.

It's Still All about You

The Rock was becoming all the Master Artist created him to be. You can too. Let the Artist paint your life with color, vibrancy and exquisiteness.

How does that happen?

Through surrender: Will you trust the Master Artist with your life?

Will you believe He can paint a better masterpiece with His brush and paint and plans, than you can with your own tools?

Go ahead and put down your brush. Let Him have the canvas to your life. Trust Him with

every

single

stroke.

Going Deeper
(To be answered individually or with a small group.)

• We all have a few regrets—things we wish we could forget or have a do-over. Is there anything in your life hindering you from being the person Jesus wants you to be?
• Read 2 Corinthians 5:17. What does this say to Christians concerning their past? How should that affect the way we approach those things?
• Sometimes in order to gain victory over our failures we need to confront them head on. Is there anything you need to do in order to gain victory over your rooster crows? Are you willing to do those things?
• Can you think of anyone in your life who may be living in defeat? What can you do to help him or her through this? Will you do it?
• Are you familiar with the old hymn "I Surrender All"? If so, sing it to yourself (or with your small group) after praying the prayer below. Make this your personal closure of your rooster crows.

"I Surrender All"
Words by J.W. Van Deventer
Music by W.S. Weeden

All to Jesus I surrender, all to Him I freely give.
I will ever love and trust Him, in His presence daily live.
I surrender all. I surrender all.
All to Thee my blessed Savior, I surrender all.

All to Jesus I surrender, Lord I give myself to Thee.
Fill me with Thy love and power; let Thy blessing fall on me.

I surrender all. I surrender all.
All to Thee my blessed Savior, I surrender all.

Prayer time: Dear Jesus, I'm tired of trying to make my life make sense.
I'm ready to trust You as the Master Artist of my life. I surrender all. I
give You my very self. I choose to live in obedience to You. I will yield
to Your authority. Please make me, mold me, reshape me into all You
want me to become. I trust You, Jesus and I love You with my life!

CHAPTER
EIGHTEEN

God created you with potential.

He has an exciting plan for your life.

He wants to use you in big ways.

We can't always see it, because we can't see the future.

But if we'll trust Him in the small, daily areas of our lives,

He'll use us in bigger ways.

The key?

Obeying even when you don't understand.

This means that sometimes the least likely win the race,

get the lead in the play and are remembered forever.

STRANGE

(Matthew 9:9; Mark 1:2-8)

Earth is a theater filled with a crowded audience.

The people are packed tightly together; expectant.

Anticipating.

You're there. Front row. Edge of your seat.

The curtains have opened.

Act One has been announced: The Beginning.

The lights shift gradually. A slight change in the hues of red and yellow. He's not in the spotlight, but he's standing inside the color formation, stage left. Before his lines are delivered, you know his role is important.

Without hesitation, right on cue, he doesn't simply *deliver* his lines, he *declares* them.

MALACHI: Behold, I send My messenger before Your face, who will prepare Your way before You.

Your eyes move to stage right where the slight change in blue and yellows directs your attention. Again, not in the spotlight, but standing near the edge of the stage, another key role. Before you have time to absorb the previous lines, the following is delivered.

ISAIAH: The voice of one crying in the wilderness: Prepare the way of the Lord! Make His paths straight!

Malachi and Isaiah's roles are complete. They've delivered the message. They've made the introduction. They now exit the stage of history and the colored hues of lights blend into one strong yellow beam. It's shining brightly on a wilderness setting and scene one begins.

The star?

No one we would have chosen. In fact, at his audition we would have been tempted to say, "Thanks, but no thanks."

Seriously?

But filling the role and now standing center stage is John the Baptist. We actually smell him before we see him. Everything about him seems strange.

Such an important role! The forerunner. The baptizer.

And given to...*him?*

We shift uncomfortably in our seats. We want a well-dressed businessman. One who's well educated in marketing. Someone who knows strategy; cause and effect; supply and demand. One who can predict trends and interpret graphs of steady growth vs. decline.

But we didn't cast the role. And like it or not, it belongs to John the Baptist.

Again, strange. Before we have a chance to think too deeply about it, however, we realize we're right inside of Mark 1:8. Right in the thick of John's introduction.

Maybe we can get used to him. Perhaps we can become comfortable together. After all, hasn't God always filled important roles with the least talented? Hasn't He always used the least expected to accomplish great things? That's one of the great benefits of being a Christ follower.

A donkey speaks to its master.

A teenage girl brings the Savior into our world.

A former Christian-killer delivers the gospel to the Gentiles.

Even so, John the Baptist may be one of the strangest. But it was Jesus Himself who declared,

"Among those born of women there has not risen one greater"
(Matthew 11:11 NKJV).

Think about that. John smells bad. He doesn't fit the mold. Or maybe he's *wearing* mold. It's hard to tell. But in plain English, he just stinks. He has no social skills. He's *different*.

And what he eats is disgusting—locusts and other crawling things. He obviously doesn't care about his appearance. He's wearing something made out of camel skin. Where are the animal rights people?

John is really, really, really different. But still, Jesus says this about him. Let's look at it again:

"Among those born of women there has not risen one greater"
(Matthew 11:11).

What a compliment! There have been a lot of compliments given throughout time. But can you think of one higher than this? Jesus said John was great! That's simply incredible. It's amazing.

I really want this in my life.

I need this in my life.

I want to be great in Jesus' eyes.

Searching

What was it about John that caused Jesus to say those words? What made John so great? I want to know the answer to those questions. I need to know the answer to those questions. Let's examine his life.

John's story is a little different. Okay, it's a lot different. His story begins in a strange way. In chapter one of Luke's gospel we meet a man and woman. Zacharias was a priest and Elizabeth was his wife.

Verse six informs us the two were both righteous and blameless before God. In other words, they were wonderful people. They were living right, serving God and others. And yet they had difficulty in their lives: They had no children and they were getting older.

We find Zacharias fulfilling his duty as a priest in the temple when the angel of the Lord, Gabriel, appears to him. Gabriel has come with a message: He and Elizabeth will have a son and name him John.

John will have an incredible purpose:

"He will bring back many of the people of Israel to the Lord their God. And he will go on before the Lord, in the spirit and power of Elijah, to turn the hearts of the parents to their children and the disobedient to the wisdom of the righteous—to make ready a people prepared for the Lord"
(Luke 1:16-17 NIV).

They would have a son! He was a promise with a purpose for the people. John was part of the plan. He was a main actor in the Divine Drama. He was the forerunner; he would actually prepare the way for the Star of the show.

God is moving. His hand was upon Zacharias, Elizabeth and John. Wow, what a strange beginning!

God's Word Is True

John is born. And the story continues...

Gabriel had said John would be great in God's sight; that he wouldn't drink wine or strong drink, and he would be filled with the Holy Spirit while still in his mother's womb. And John lives his life true to Gabriel's words. As he grows, though, we notice he chooses a strange dwelling.

John removes himself from all the comforts of society. He chooses to be a desert dweller. He lives in a hot, wild place. His home is the wilderness, away from the city and some 1,300 feet below sea level.

This is where he sets up shop; where he starts his church. By his location we can see what his desire is. He takes his calling seriously. He determines he will have an impact on society, not the other way around. It was a complete separation. He was separated from the trappings of the world and culture, but separated unto God. Remember, he was a promise with a purpose for the people. John had a strange dwelling.

Not the Right Label

Not only were his beginnings and dwelling strange, remember again his dress. Mark 1:6 tells us, "John was clothed in camel hair." Not cotton. Not satin or silk. Not even wool or polyester. Camel hair with a leather belt around his waist! How do you clean a camel-haired wrap? You don't. Now we're back to smelling him before we see him. *Strange.*

But wait, we're not finished. Let's take a closer peek at his diet: "…and he ate locusts and wild honey." Imagine talking with John one on one. Lingering in the air you smell the scent of fresh honey. When John smiles, perhaps you notice a grasshopper leg twitching between his front teeth!

John had a strange dwelling.

Strange dress.

Strange diet.

And he also had a strange message. In fact, this was actually the motivation behind everything else he did.

This message burned in his bones.

It made his heart beat.

It flowed inside his veins.

It was his very purpose. He was preparing the way. He would stand on the banks of the river in the wilderness and challenge people to change their lives. He urged them to repent—literally walk away from sinful actions—and get ready for the coming Promise.

This message—it was as much of his life as breathing—he

couldn't hold back. Like a bulldozer moving stubborn earth, John exploded through the multitudes.

He detonated the high places; filling in the low, straightening out the crooked. John advanced, as a scout would run before an accelerating army to inform for safe passage. He moved, as a footman would run before the chariot of the king to ensure safe, smooth, quick travel for the elite.

John leveled the paths to make ready for the One coming. Anything that would stand in the way of this happening would have to be dealt with. He would call the people, pauper or prince, no matter what price to him, to turn from an old way of life to embrace the new. He was the scout, the footman, the forerunner: Preparing the way for the Promise—the Christ.

John's message was unlike any other. It was, you guessed it, strange.

The Crowds

And yet this strange message draws a strange response! People come in multitudes to hear John preach with boldness. They were hungry for the truth. They'd waited a long time to hear from God. They were yearning for His voice.

As we end the Old Testament by closing the last page of Malachi and before we begin the New Testament by opening the first page of Matthew, to read that a Savior has come, we find ourselves locked inside a 400-year-vault of absolute silence from God.

Four hundred years!

Not a prophet had been raised up.

Only a holy hush wrapping itself around humanity.

Now that John the Baptist is on center stage prophesying the Promised One, the people are anxious to hear more.

So they come to him. This was no easy task. John's schedule wasn't advertised. There were no marquees outside the temple announcing, "Tonight at 7 p.m., John the Baptizer will be speaking."

He wasn't in the cities. John wasn't traveling from location to location with this message.

There was no tour.

No rallies.

No conferences or sold-out arenas.

John didn't go to the crowds. The crowds came to him. Mark 1:5 gives us the snapshot:

"Then all the land of Judea, and those from Jerusalem, went out to him."

This took a lot of effort.

First they had to find him! Remember, he's somewhere in the wilderness. And he's 1,300 feet below sea level. It was a long, arduous journey. Yet multitudes were willing to make the trip to hear this strange man, with a strange beginning, in a strange dwelling with a strange look, proclaiming a strange message.

Why?

It's amazing what we'll do for truth. And we all want it. Everyone's seeking it. Even Pilate asked about it: "What is truth?" (See John 18:38.) Through the years, the quest hasn't changed.

We're still seeking truth.

We want it.

We need it.

Everything within our molecular structure yearns for it.

We have to have it.

John was intent on sharing it. Yes, in a strange way. But still truth, nonetheless.

But let's not get lost in the details. Let's remember why we're examining his story. It's because Jesus said he was great, remember?

That's why we started this journey.

Again, I want to know…

I need to know…

Is the secret to his greatness found in his beginnings? The fact that the Holy Spirit was given to him when he was still inside his mother's womb? If so, there's no hope for me. I wasn't born that way. That can't be it.

Is the secret found in his dwelling? If so, then I'm willing to move to the wilderness. I'll go to the desert. I want to be great in Jesus' sight.

Thankfully, that's not it either.

Is it in his dress? If so, point me to the camel skin outlet.

His diet? I don't know how they'd taste, but I'm game! I'll try a serving a locust crepes.

Is it the message? I'll call people a "brood of vipers" like he did.

Though all these things are interesting, none of them are what made John great! And this could possibly be the strangest thing about his story—John had a strange characteristic.

Let's Look Even Deeper

When we examine John's life—when we place it under a microscope and look at it closer than we ever hope anyone looks at ours—it seems as though he lived it all for one moment. It's a moment that's recorded in the Gospel of John 1:29-34.

John the Baptist has been fulfilling his purpose down in the Jordan River. There have been steady crowds of people coming to him, responding to his message. But today something different is about to happen. John senses it.

He looks up and sees the silhouette of a man. There's something about this man. It's what he's been waiting for. John sees Jesus. He lifts his hand from the river, still dripping with water, and he points at the Christ. In a loud, demonstrative voice, he proclaims, "Behold! The Lamb of God! Who takes away the sin of the world!"

Can you hear the excitement in his proclamation?

"This is the One I've been telling you about! This is the One we've been looking for! This is the One we've been waiting for! This is all about Him! Behold the Lamb of God! He will take away your sins and give you eternal life. Wholeness."

Amazing.

John's strange characteristic?

He lived his entire life pointing to Jesus.

Remember: John was a promise with a purpose for the people. And in that promise he would point to the Person. It was all about Jesus.

Why is that so amazing? Think about it. John had it all. They were coming to *him*. He had a following, a name. He could have had anything he wanted in the world. And yet, when others thought he was the one, he pointed them to Jesus.

In fact, these are his words:

> "He must increase, but I must decrease"
> (John 3:30 NKJV).

When it could have been all about him, he made it all about Jesus. He longed for no popularity. He wasn't seeking fame.

He *lived* to point others to Jesus.

That was his heartbeat.

His mindset.

His life.

That's just strange. It goes against our nature.

But it's what made John so great.

Putting It All Together

Remember why we started the journey?

I want to know.

I need to know.

Here it is. If I want to be great, I may have to be strange. I have to live my life in such a way that I'm constantly pointing others to Jesus.

The world is filled with a whole lot of people living for a whole lot of things. If I want to be great in Jesus' eyes, I must live my life as a proclamation of "Behold the Lamb of God."

This is what life is all about.

This is what gives life meaning.

In less, we find more.

In death we find life.

If we really want to live, we have to lose our lives in Him.

Pointing others to Jesus.

I want this in my life.

I need this in my life.

It's strange, but God uses strange people to accomplish His purposes in this world.

Are you willing to be used by Him in ways that seem strange?

From Susie:

I consider Stephane the sister I never had. She's actually

my sister-in-law, but besides being intimate friends, I think of her as my sister. Not too long ago, one of her dear friends Jane, was in the hospital battling cancer. Steph began praying diligently for her and visiting her in the hospital. One day while Steph was at the mall, she noticed a kiosk selling sock monkey hats and a variety of other cute animal hats with the fun, long braids on each side, and she immediately thought of Jane's gregarious, outgoing personality.

"The sock monkey hat especially grabbed my attention," she said. "It was adorable." As she picked up the hat and turned it over in her hands, she felt strongly impressed to buy it. "I was wondering if it was one of those God-impressions," she says. "It was so strange; I was guessing that it had to be from God. The longer I held the hat, I sensed Him telling me to buy it for Jane. But it just didn't make sense. I knew she had lost her hair, and I didn't want to offend her by making her think she should cover her head."

Steph resisted the urge to purchase the hat and went home. But the impression continued to resonate in her mind. She couldn't forget about the sock monkey hat. "But again, because this was such a strange impression, I just kept thinking I was crazy."

As the days passed, however, the impression just got stronger. "I kept praying about it and finally realized I needed to go back and purchase the hat." About a week later, Steph found herself at the same kiosk handling the sock monkey hat. The impression was still there. She bought the hat and took it home.

"I just kept looking at the hat I'd purchased," she said, "and asked the Lord if I had done the right thing. It seemed such a *strange* thing to do! Even though I now *had* the hat, I couldn't bring myself to give it to her."

A few more days passed, and the impression had become so strong, Steph knew she could no longer ignore it. "I grabbed the hat and put it in a fun little gift bag and decided to give it to her husband so he could take it to her. He works about a block from where I do, so I took it to his office.

"I stood across from his desk with the bag at my feet so he couldn't see it. Even though I had no doubt by this time the impression was from God, I was still leery of giving him the hat."

They made small talk for a while, and in the middle of their conversation he received a phone call from the hospital. His wife was on the line. "I couldn't help, but hear his end of the conversation," Steph says.

"Okay. I'll get one. I'm leaving in just a few minutes. Yes, I know where to get it. I'll be there shortly," he said.

He hung up the phone and looked at Stephane. "That was Jane," he said. "She has lost all her hair, and her head gets so cold in the hospital. She wants me to get her a hat." Shaking his head and chuckling he said, "She's very specific about what she wants. She told me to go to the mall and get her one of those crazy sock monkey hats."

Steph reached down and grabbed the bag. "Randy, you don't have to go to the mall. You don't have to buy a crazy sock monkey hat. It's right here. Tell Jane we love her, we're praying for her, and that God is so very faithful."

God uses people sometimes in strange ways…to do strange things…to accomplish His will.

Are you willing to be used by Him in ways that may seem strange?

Are you ready to go against the crowd?

If so, you have the makings of a disciple.

Once you accept His love,

    His forgiveness,

        His restoration…

you receive the benefit of being in His Kingdom:

    living an empowered life through His Spirit,

        living with peace and purpose,

            living focused on Him instead of you.

You see, from the disciple's perspective, it becomes all about the Father.

The created desiring to please the Creator.

The canvas reflecting the image of the Artist.

All the Father has done has been motivated by His love for you:

His departure from a grandiose and perfect Kingdom to walk and live in your world.

His pursuit of you, His restoration of you, even His death and resurrection were for *you.*

The Artist came to restore.

To heal. To make whole.

To breathe fresh paint into your weary soul.

It's *you* on the canvas.

From His perspective it will always be about you.

But now that you're a Christ-follower, from your perspective, it becomes all about Him.

He's your reason for living. He's the air you breathe. He becomes your heartbeat. He's the blood flowing through your veins, the marrow in your bones. He's not simply an important part of your life, He *becomes* your life.

How will others know that you're a disciple?

They'll know by your perspective. They'll see it in your actions. They're watching the canvas.

And they'll notice your willingness to be used in strange ways.

Going Deeper

(To be answered individually or with a small group.)

- What are three benefits in being a Christ follower?
- Can you describe a time when someone did something that seemed strange to him or her, but it was exactly what you needed?
- Identify a time in your own life when you were willing to do something that seemed strange because you felt impressed by God to do so.
- John the Baptist was intently focused on Christ. What would need to change in your life for you to become this focused?
- We *could* say John was obsessed with Christ. He lived for Him, thought about Him 24/7, separated himself from anyone and anything that would distract Him from Christ, and made Him the topic of every conversation. Is there anyone like that in your world today? Can you describe someone who fits this description?
- John knew he had to distance himself from distractions, so he lived in the wilderness. Though God doesn't call every Christian to live in the wilderness, He *does* want our full attention. What are some common spiritual distractions you face?
- Is it possible to distance yourself from some of the distractions that keep you from becoming all Christ wants you to be? What specifically would you need to do?
- Read John 15:19. What does this Scripture have to say about being part of this world?
- Now read Romans 12:2. How can we be in the world, but not of the world?
- Is your life all about you? Or have you committed yourself wholly to Jesus Christ? According to Matthew 16:25, you must lose your life to find it.

Prayer time: Dear Jesus, I'm willing to lose my life in You. I want to follow You, obey You, and point others to You. Make me keenly aware of the things that hinder—or distract—me from becoming all You want me to be. As you bring these things to my mind, I will commit them to You. I'm willing to be seen as "strange" or different. I simply want to become all You desire me to be.

MASTERPIECE

Made in the USA
San Bernardino, CA
12 July 2015